The Birth of the Modern Mind

The Birth
of the Modern Mind

Self, Consciousness,
and the Invention of
the Sonnet

Paul Oppenheimer

New York · Oxford
OXFORD UNIVERSITY PRESS
1989

Oxford University Press

Oxford   New York   Toronto
Delhi   Bombay   Calcutta   Madras   Karachi
Petaling Jaya   Singapore   Hong Kong   Tokyo
Nairobi   Dar es Salaam   Cape Town
Melbourne   Auckland

and associated companies in
Berlin   Ibadan

Library of Congress Cataloging-in-Publication Data

Oppenheimer, Paul.
  The birth of the modern mind : self, consciousness, and the
invention of the sonnet / Paul Oppenheimer.
     p.   cm.
  Bibilography: p.
  Includes index.
  ISBN 0–19–505692–2
  1. Sonnet.   2. Sonnets, European—History and criticism.
3. Literature, Modern—History and criticism.   I. Title.
PN1514.06   1989   88–23819
809.1′42—dc 19   CIP

9 8 7 6 5 4 3 2 1

Printed in the United States of America
on acid-free paper

To my mother and father

Preface

This book presents new discoveries about the thought and literature that may be termed "modern" and their development. The
usual place for discoveries is certainly the scholarly journal, where
evidence and references may be set out together, and that was the
forum chosen for my essay "The Origin of the Sonnet," which
appeared in the journal *Comparative Literature* in 1982, and
which, with various changes, is included here as Part III. Nonetheless, it seems to me that new facts and ideas may demand new
means of illustration and clarification, which might also make
them available to the public at large. A book of this type seems
appropriate. In it, the sonnet's true importance in the history
of human development, and the implications of its importance,
can be broadly explored and evaluated. A fresh account of the
birth of literature and literary tradition in the West can be advanced, together with a new understanding of Dante's role, as
well as the role of Giacomo da Lentino, who invented the sonnet,
in creating very modern styles of thought. The historical background and its flavor can be better understood and described.
Through translations of European sonnets spanning seven centuries, additional evidence can be offered, revealing how modern
thought and literature began and changed over time, and by implication how English, and later American, literature changed
along similar lines. The nature of the translations, for the most
part of poems not previously rendered into English, is taken up in
the Note on the Translations. For the moment, it may be enough
to say that I have chosen to translate these particular poems in the
belief that they provide a clear lens through which to view the expansion of human perceptions of reality since the *duecento,* or
what we call the thirteenth century.

I am grateful to many colleagues and friends in the Department
of English of The City College of New York for support and sug-

gestions, among them Saul Brody, Frederick Goldin, Leo Hama-
lian, Norman Kelvin, Valerie Krishna, Barbara Fisher, and Barry
Wallenstein. I wish to thank the editors of *Comparative Literature*
for allowing me to reprint, with alterations, my article "The Origin
of the Sonnet," from vol. 34, no. 4 (Fall 1982), and Sidney
Feshbach, the editor of *Rough Translations,* for permission to
reprint two of my translations of poems, by Giacomo da Lentino
and Rainer Maria Rilke. The cooperation of Insel Verlag, whose
texts of Rilke's "Dame vor dem Spiegel," "Gesang der Frauen an
den Dichter," "Der Tod des Dichters," "Der Tod der Geliebten,"
and "Archäischer Torso Apollos" are reprinted here, is also appreciated, as is that of ECON Verlag for the text and English-
translation rights to "Geduld," by Marie Louise Kaschnitz. The
debt I owe to numbers of scholars, while acknowledged by cita-
tions in Parts I and III and in the Bibliography, extends far past
the capacity of any citation to do it justice. Much of my work was
done in the collections of the library of The City College of New
York and The New York Public Library, and I am delighted to
recall the generous assistance of their staffs. Angus Fletcher and
Michael Shute provided advice and encouragement that were
deeply needed. Harry Rolnick did the same. I am grateful to my
editor and publisher for being willing to reproduce various minia-
tures from *De arte venandi cum avibus,* by Frederick II (Codex
Ms. Pal. Lat. 1071 of the Vatican Library, as taken from the
facsimile edition of this volume by Akademische Druck- und Verlagsanstalt, Graz, 1969). I owe much in the way of encouragement
and patience to my two children, Julie and Ben. My greatest debt
of gratitude is owed to two special friends, Andras Hamori and
Francesca Simpson Pedler, who read the manuscript and showed
me where and how it might be improved. Their help has been
invaluable. With wit and spirit they kept me in mind of the fact
that scholarly detective work and translation are above all mis-
sions of love.

New York   P.O.
May 1988

Contents

I

*The Birth
of the Modern Mind:
New Facts and a Theory*

Inception and Background

Modern thought and literature begin with the invention of the sonnet. Created in the early *duecento* by Giacomo da Lentino, a *notaro*, or important court official and probably lawyer at the court of the emperor Frederick II, it is the first lyric form since the fall of the Roman Empire intended not for music or performance but for silent reading.[1] As such, it is the first lyric of self-consciousness, or of the self in conflict. The sonnet's peculiar fourteen-line structure, which has intrigued countless poets ever since—the sonnet remains to this day the oldest poetic form still in wide popular use—is traceable to Plato's *Timaeus*, with its mathematical description of the architecture of the human soul and of heaven. The sonnet seeks to catch and echo the melodies "unheard" of the human soul, to use Keats' phrase, melodies both passionate and silent, both intimate and celestial.

Given its fresh and deep appeal, it should come as no surprise that the sonnet immediately caught on, thrilling poets of the clever *scuola siciliana* surrounding Frederick and influencing poets of the *dolce stil nuovo,* such as Dante and Petrarch. Frederick himself wrote a number of sonnets, and his brilliant court, which resounded with intellectual argument and fervor, the fervor of the incipient Renaissance, the rediscovery of the classics and of ancient and buried ideas, produced many of them. The new form was quickly understood as a new way of thinking about mankind. Emotional problems, especially problems in love, needed no longer merely be expressed or performed: they might now actually be resolved, or provisionally resolved, through the logic of a form that turned expression inward,[2] to a resolution in the abiding peace of the soul itself, or if one were not so certain of the existence of

1. The proofs of these assertions are presented in Part III. Part I, with its theory, is an expansion of conclusions reached there.
2. See Part III, pp. 182–84.

3

the soul, in reason. Reason, after all, was perceived as a manifestation of God's mind and of divine love. Ptolemy, and his system of describing the known universe, coupled neatly with the theology of Saint Augustine and Boethius, had long since made that clear, ever since the fifth century. All medieval art, music, architecture, science, and literature were based on it. Reason, as announced by the orderliness of the heavens and Church philosophy, reigned supreme.

On the other hand, the idea of turning inward, implicit in the form of the sonnet, contained a dangerous question, one that had not seriously been raised since Roman times. If poets asked about their values, their being, their ontology, which the form seemed to require, would the results harmonize with Church teachings and what was generally known about the world? To understand this question fully, the contents of the fashionable Provençal love lyrics and other love poetry of Giacomo's day must be distinguished from the "mad," fascinating contents of the new sonnets. In fact, Giacomo's accomplishment, and his influence on the literature around him, and indirectly over the next seven hundred years, cannot really be grasped without knowing something of the cultural landscape against which he worked. The important feature here, both in the poetry and the landscape, is what might be called "distance," especially in the poetry. This too is ultimately traceable to the Ptolemaic system, with its ideas of reason, or God, in which everybody believed.

Provençal courtly love poetry, the poetry of *fin amour,* had been popular in France and elsewhere in Europe since the twelfth century. Often composed in lengthy strophes, or stanzas, with complex meters and rhyme schemes, and intended to be sung, usually by the poet-composer-musician himself, it was a poetry of the noble classes. Frequently, poets were themselves knights, kings, or in some cases noblewomen. Their poetry, which was thus clearly meant for public entertainment before a highly sophisticated group, made fashionable a love relationship, or courtly love situation, which possessed certain unusual and deliberately artificial qualities. In these poems the lover—invariably the singer-poet—found himself far from his "goal," most likely a married woman of the same class, though she might on occasion occupy a higher station at some court than he did. The poet's "distance" from his beloved, in what usually amounted to a lover's triangle, was reinforced by her conventional rejection of his advances, as well as his despair and persistence. He might present himself as contemptuous of her scorn, as in the earthy lyrics of Guillaume IX, or desolate, as in the haunting *canzoni* of the twelfth-century poet Cercamon, but his pose was always that of the lover denied, the lover struggling to prove himself worthy through feats of arms, the lover as martyr for love, even, and perhaps especially, for the idea of love. The most important feature of the relationship, however, was its glorious intended artificiality. Courtly love poetry presents, often brilliantly, a splendid vacuity. Actual people nearly never wander through it. If a name is mentioned, it is clearly a stock name, a "Jack" or "Jill," not that of the true lover, who might be sitting in at a performance, and whose embarrassment, considering the delicacy of the situation, was to be avoided at all costs. The poet-singer himself was scarcely more fleshed out in his own work. He became what scholars such as W. T. H. Jackson have described as a lover-poet-performer-persona as he sang, revealing less of his personal attitudes and feelings, or for that matter biography, than exploring afresh, and if possible with dazzling polish, an exciting state of mind, a delicious longing. He was the poet of silver emptiness. His soul, decorated with unimaginable sorrows, became a refined music and an exquisite paean of words for all to hear, while his truest, deepest personal torments were kept hidden. On the few occasions when they were mentioned, as in the related *Minnesang* lyrics of Walther von der Vogelweide, the language and phrases used to describe them were of an instantly recognizable conventional type, one that added to the audience's sense of illusion and "distance." Such poetry possessed, and possesses, a deep attraction, for it was tantalizingly private as well as public. The fashion for it persists in altered forms into our own day. Many modern love songs, with their themes of rejection and a near-religious adoration of a beloved and often absent woman or man, echo the plaints, if less often the wit, of Provençal court performers.

All this theatrical type of poetry had a good deal in common with the Ptolemaic system and the prevalent theology that became attached to it, even if the poetry was not demonstrably and directly derived from what either Ptolemy or the Catholic theologians actually believed, or wished people to think. Ptolemy, a quite accomplished mathematician, astronomer, geographer, and cartographer of second-century Alexandria, had worked from observations of the planets and stars as old as the Babylonians, seventeen-hundred years earlier than he, and come up with a design of the physical universe. When Ptolemy's design was combined with Aristotelian physics, Platonic idealism, Augustinian ethics, and Boethius' vision of how God operated through logic, the result was a complete explanation of phenomena everywhere in creation. Everything physical, mental, and spiritual, including disease and disaster, was comprehensible according to this system. Everything not explained by it simply did not exist, or was regarded as untrue or illusionary. Mankind had achieved total knowledge, or so it was felt.

Ptolemy's system of nine spheres emphasized humanity's distance from the creating mind of God, called the Empyrean, and was above all not anthropocentric. It was a study in order and loss. This is a fact not sufficiently appreciated, even by historians of science. A glance at a model of the Ptolemaic spheres shows the earth at what looks like the static center of a finite and round universe. The truth, though, discoverable in medieval literature as well as in various papal bulls and theological treatises (by Anselm, Aquinas, and Joachim de Flora, for instance), is that the huge numbers of people who thought of themselves as living in a "middle age," or *status mediocris,* believed that they inhabited a "wretched" wasteland stuck at the bottom of everything that God had created. What looks like the center, to the modern observer, appeared to them to be a nearly desolate, and certainly most inferior, corner of things. Far from being at any "center," mankind was almost abandoned. It is significant, as C. S. Lewis has pointed out in his fine study of the medieval model, *The Discarded Image* (Cambridge, Eng. 1964), that when Mary, the mother of Christ, is blessed by an angel at the Annunciation, she is visited only by an archangel. Archangels belonged to the eighth, or next to lowest category, in an hierarchy of nine types of angels, or species of divine energy, thought to swarm and sing and govern in the spaces between Ptolemy's spheres.

If one great theme of this sort of universe was the vast distance from God—understood as the creative intelligence surrounding the physical envelope of things—other themes were its descending order, termed "naturalness" by Aristotle, and salvation through faith. The distance from God, it was believed, had left men and women irrational, for they were "a little lower than the angels," both spiritually and intellectually. The near disconnection from divine reason, across space, explained the "madness" of most human activities and human history, in which blind instinct and mere appetite held sway. On the other hand, the distance might be overcome, through devotion, good works, and prayer. This was especially true if one were a saint. For more ordinary mortals, a quite real terror and a sense that bodily life was intrinsically worthless, along with a perception of God's reason as a frightening type of love, led to a conviction of personal futility, often expressed in the literature. Dream visions such as *Pearl,* in Middle English (ca. 1375), reveal a common understanding of life itself as empty, and death as a possible gateway to heaven, or the city of God's reason, albeit in quite dazzling poetry.

Hierarchical feudalistic society mirrored these ideas of abandonment, distance, and salvation through faith or loyalty—what Chaucer terms *trouthe.* The king, or queen, resembled the "distant" intelligence or God of the universe, bestowing himself and his power on his subjects as from a divine height. The king's role was less that of master among servants than of superior being among inferiors. His superiority, it was believed, was guaranteed physically through excellent inherited genes. These perpetuated an ancient royal connection to God Himself, in a mysterious fashion never fully explained in the texts on the "divine right of kings." Royal genes also implied—there was no guarantee here—that while the society over which the king ruled might be ruled cruelly, and certainly unfairly, yet it would be ruled as God might rule it, with some sort of justice. The widespread belief that this was the case accounts for the centuries required to overthrow surviving European monarchies, following the Middle Ages. The conviction that kings and queens were genetically different from everybody else, and that even the aristocratic classes were biologically different from peasants and artisans, led to the stubborn refusal of masses of people to accept Darwin's theory of evolution, even some six hundred years after Giacomo da Lentino invented the sonnet. When Louis XVI announced, as he went to the guillotine in 1793, "Après moi, le déluge," he meant that the mob about to assume power in France did not, by his lights, consist of human beings. A willingness by otherwise gallant medieval rulers, such as Richard *Coeur de Lion,* to use peasants' heads as cannonballs in bombarding castles during sieges, resulted less from contempt for the peasants than from an unshakable conviction that peasants simply belonged to a lower species of animal, a bit like dogs (which Descartes described as "machines" without true emotions, as late as the seventeenth century).

It is arguably more difficult to eliminate rational but false beliefs about reality than to explode superstitions, and as may be imagined, the Middle Ages were above all rational. They were apparently more committed to reason than our own age. Modern science, while aspiring to reason, acknowledges the biases of investigators and observers. Disputes often arise over the possibly "spontaneous" behavior of certain strata of subatomic reality. But medieval people—in Europe, North Africa, the Middle East, and parts of Asia, in societies Christian and Moslem and Jewish, all sharing the same ideas about the physical if not the spiritual universe—disbelieved most powerfully in any possible physical irrationality. That God was reason incarnate, that mere man inhabited an abandoned ignorant place quite far from Him and below Him, seemed obvious to everyone. Nor was this a "superstitious" conviction. It was felt that Ptolemy had demonstrated its truth with mathematics and observation, and that Boethius had confirmed it with irrefutable logic. God was thought to be a Word, or *verbum,* in the Latin commonly used by educated people, an abstraction, an a priori Being. God was previous to the physical, and drastically different from it. Saint John had announced this important premise in his first-century gospel: "In the beginning was the Word; and the Word was with God; and the Word was God." Statements such as these were hardly convenient metaphors. They were understood as precise descriptions of the divine reality that had preceded creation and that continued into the present, the "middle age."

These ideas—of God, of kings, of social relations, and of the physical universe—are echoed, if not directly copied out, in the love lyrics of the troubadours of Provence. The "distant," scornful Lady, who is to be wooed with the words of the love-lost singer-poet-persona, mimics in the flesh the abstract and abandoning God, who is to be placated with prayer. What is more, it is evident that the poet who is to win her, like the pious man in search of salvation, must look outward, abandoning himself, his ego, and his doubts about the world, if he is to succeed. He is to avoid self-consciousness.

But most writers of the period, along with their audiences of whatever class, were already quite accustomed to ignoring the "self," in the modern sense of a personality in conflict. Centuries of medieval allegory, in painting, drama, and other literary genres, had habituated people to the idea of the externalized conflict, in which human emotions and qualities—such as wrath, love, strength, and piety—were personified and shown in complexly plotted debates and struggles. *Le Roman de la Rose,* of the twelfth century, represents a perfection of this art form in the High Middle Ages, while Spenser's *Faerie Queene* demonstrates a lingering affection for it in the Renaissance. The tradition of this sort of allegory reaches at least back to Prudentius, the Spanish-Christian poet of the fourth century, whose pagan imagery (of the Winged Victory figure, for instance) belies a popular enthusiasm for assimilating the old Roman religion of gods and goddesses to a rapidly expanding Christianity. At all events, it is clear that allegorical literature, as majestic and vigorous as it was impersonal, appealed strongly to the founders of the Church. In the early centuries of Church history, clerical support for it even invited violence—which also received strong official support. Robert Holland Smith, in his essay *The Death of Classical Paganism* (New York, 1976), has shown that by suppressing and burning Greek and Roman literature the early Church fathers guaranteed the spread of medieval allegory. This opened a new era. Promoting allegory was of importance in ensuring a new fashion of relying on an institution, the Church itself, rather than on introspection or self-questioning, or even on a personal communion with God, for one's happiness, or as one passed through life's more bitter moments.

As a result, the differences between classical and medieval European literature are striking. The self-consciousness of a Sophoclean Oedipus, not to mention Homer's Odysseus and the works of Virgil, Tacitus, Plautus, Sappho, and Seneca, is almost universally absent in the European literature of the seven centuries after the fall of Rome. While this difference is not terribly puzzling, in view of Church suppression of classical literature and the approval of allegory, it should be clearly understood.

In Sophocles' *Oedipus Rex,* to cite a well known instance, the conflict may be said to be internal because it occurs within the mind of the hero and because its solution is also to be found there. Both facts are crucial. Oedipus, as king of the city of Thebes, knows at the outset of Sophocles' tragedy that responsibility rests with him for ending the plague that is killing off his subjects. Oedipus knows this because he knows and subscribes to a traditional Greek view of kingship, according to which the welfare of the state lies absolutely in his hands. Whether the plague proves in the end to have been "caused" by acts of his own is of less importance. He knows that he must put a stop to it, and that no one else can do so. His subjects assume, moreover, that he must either have angered the gods, and thus be a direct cause of the calamity, or committed a crime leading to the same result. In assuming this, they turn out to be right, but again, the point is not so much whether they are right. The real question is that of Oedipus' responsibility. It is his sense of responsibility that leads to his self-knowledge and self-consciousness.

Oedipus does not immediately realize, of course, that he has murdered his father and married his mother, crimes which—along with a prophecy at birth that he would do so—have produced his horrifying situation. Again, in the Greek scheme of things, this is of little importance. Innocence counts for nothing here; responsibility, and the courage to transform catastrophe into rescue, count for everything. They become the measure of Oedipus as tragic hero. When Oedipus sets about investigating the murder of the previous king, Laius, aware that in solving this mystery he will also solve the mystery of the plague, the play becomes a quite modern detective story, with the curious and frightening twist that the detective uncovers his own guilt. But once more, the important issue is that Oedipus' frustration in being unable to fulfill his responsibility as king leads to his understanding himself, to his finally seeing himself as an incestuous regicide. Freud has remarked that frustration is the beginning of self-consciousness. To this it might be added that the self-conscious process probably leads to mature insights only if one refuses to blame others for one's condition. Oedipus notably refuses to do so.

It is a far cry from the frustration of Oedipus—or of Catullus in his tormented, self-conscious love lyrics—to the amazing and easy ignorance of self to be found in the medieval *Everyman* (ca. 1475; a Dutch version, *Elckerlijc,* is almost certainly earlier), or in the twelfth-century Middle High German epic *Parzival,* by Wolfram von Eschenbach. The theme of both works, which may be seen as representative of medieval beliefs about the internal human world, is that self-ignorance may be overcome through an acknowledgement of God, or the larger universe. Informed that he is about to die, Everyman prepares for his "journey" as he would for any journey, by packing and looking for traveling companions. He knows nothing about the "journey" of death because he has never considered life, or "examined" his own life, in Socrates' phrase for self-consciousness. The play dramatizes Everyman's discovery that his "goods" cannot be taken on this particular "journey," which is grimly unique. Neither can Strength, Knowledge, Discretion, Beauty, Kinship, or Friendship. Only Good Deeds agrees to accompany him, and this after Everyman undergoes rituals with Confession and penance (all but penance, a jewel, are personified on the stage; the theater becomes an externalization of Everyman's mind, in which the audience is situated). Interestingly, from a modern or classical Greek and Roman perspective, Everyman is shown as achieving self-knowledge not by finally looking inward, as does Oedipus (or Odysseus, who is guided by Athena to examine his desertion of his wife and people), but by looking outward.

The same holds true in *Parzival.* Wolfram's masterpiece, a sort of early *Bildungsroman,* or educational novel, presents us with a hero who initially knows nothing of himself, or the knighthood he wins, or the holy grail he seeks, or anything else, and who is also something of a fool. Parzival's shattering ignorance swamps him with blunders. Led into the castle of the Fisher King, who guards the grail, Parzival is too polite and vain to ask about the king's obvious suffering. Shown the magnificent and shining grail, which is borne in a procession of ethereal women, Parzival pays no attention. He has no idea what the grail is supposed to look like,

and no curiosity. When he finds himself abandoned in a magical
wasteland the next morning—a punishment for his insensitivity—
he reflects for the first time on his human failure, but it is to take a
great deal of instruction in spiritual matters and years of knightly
combat for him to mature enough to win his way back to the
Fisher King's castle and to lay claim, rightfully at last, to the
grail. Parzival's growth into a full character, which is astonishing
and ultimately satisfying, comes about, as does Everyman's,
through an outward turning and the acceptance of heavenly guidance. A spiritually vital universe instructs both. Their final experiences are not of self-consciousness but of knowledge of God.
Allegory and a spiritual education have replaced internal aware-
ness.

It was all this that the little sonnet, often disparaged and never
clearly understood as the fulcrum for modern literature that it
was to become, affected so decisively. *Everyman, Parzival,* the
lyrics of the troubadours, and all other medieval poems were
meant to be performed. The sonnet was not. It was meant as a
meditation, as an instrument of self-reflection. Ironically, it was
invented at the court of a man of action as well as meditation,
who was himself to challenge the papacy and to herald an age in
which the personalities of individuals would be more highly es-
teemed than institutions. In this sense, and others, Frederick II
was the first truly "modern" ruler.

Frederick II, Giacomo da Lentino, and the Earliest Sonnets

The personality of Frederick II (1194–1250) is probably the key to his spectacular accomplishments, which in some cases (such as his encouragement of the sonnet) endure straight into modern times.[3] His failures, too, were spectacular, with equally long-lasting effects. Had he succeeded, for example, in his attempt to destroy the political and military alliances of the pope—his ambition for decades—he would have united Italy and Germany, certainly changing the course of European history, and possibly the world's too, over the next seven centuries. It may nonetheless be fair to say that modern intellectual life, beginning at his court and at the universities that he founded and financed, and rippling north through Italy and then in waves across the continent of Europe, continues to owe him an enormous debt.

The few flimsy and tattered likenesses that survive suggest a sultry brilliance. The erotic and sensual mingle freely with the aloof and imperial in his face. He had curly red hair and blue-green eyes—marked, some said, by a sensitive ruthlessness traceable to his grandfather, the German Frederick Barbarossa (Frederick I), whose passion for assassinating friends and enemies alike had earned him a thunderous notoriety. Frederick II was of medium height, and when a young man, before he turned stout, good looking (his good looks may have come from his mother, Queen Constance of Sicily, who died when the future emperor was four). He was precocious, learning six languages, including Arabic, in childhood, and quite early acquiring his lifelong tastes for hunting, riding, warfare, ideas, literature, conversation, and women. Growing up in Sicily, he also came intimately to understand vari-

---

3. Further comments on Frederick are to be found in Part III, pp. 185–86.

ous cultures often perceived as contradictory. Sicily at this time was a grand crossroads of Normans, Arabs, Jews, Byzantines, Saracens, Greeks, and intellectuals from all over western Europe. The open-mindedness, anticlericalism, and scientific curiosity that were to be the hallmarks of Frederick's adulthood were no doubt acquired in the freewheeling atmosphere of this relatively small mid-Mediterranean island, with its echoes of ancient civilizations, its beauties of mountains and valleys full of game, and its countless mythic ghosts. In Frederick's day, Pan's pipes might still be heard, if one listened carefully to the folksongs of peasant farmers, along-side the pious Christian hymns of hope for Christ's second coming.

He was a man of agreeable paradoxes. What else to make of a young leader who managed to have himself proclaimed emperor of Germany before learning the language? Or who, while excom-municated (he was excommunicated three times), undertook a crusade and issued his orders in the name of Jesus Christ (the pope's name being barred to him)? Or who succeeded in his crusade, and not by fighting but by flattering his Arab and Egyp-tian enemies with gifts, having at his disposal only a weak army suffering from starvation? Or who late in life conducted a siege both by walling up the citizens of the town he wished to capture—Parma—and then building an alternative town nearby, out of wood, complete with streets, houses, plumbing, water mills, gar-dens, vineyards, moats, drawbridges, orchards for his Saracen harem, a library, and a chapel? Or who busied himself during the siege not so much with military matters as with trying to finish a scientific treatise on the habits of birds?

Frederick's treatise on birds, *De arte venandi cum avibus* (*On the Art of Hunting with Birds*), survives in an illuminated copy ironically located in the Vatican Library—ironically because while revealing the depth and originality of the emperor's interests, it represented a profound threat to the established clerical model of nature. The book is far more than a discourse by Europe's most brilliant medieval ruler on his favorite sport, hunting with falcons. It is a sumptuously illustrated encyclopedia, the world's first, on the qualities, needs, and habits of many types of birds, from storks and ducks through falcons and swallows.[4] It is one of

4. See Figs. 1–3.

the first modern scientific texts, whose frank empiricism and disavowal of earlier authorities were to shatter the widespread conviction that Ptolemy's system of the spheres, Aristotle's *Physics,* and Church theology had more or less explained everything under the sun. "Our work," writes Frederick, "is to present things that are as they are." The startling quality of this statement becomes clear when one realizes that in thirteenth-century Europe it was virtual anathema to present things as they were, or to rely on sense data to do so. The theology and popular belief of the time rejoiced in describing things, or animals, or birds, not as they were but in terms of their relations to the mind of God, or biblical texts, which were assumed to be indexes to God's mind and the meanings of things. All things, and animals, were seen as spiritually meaningful. It was the duty of anyone describing them to tell the "truth" about them. The "truth" consisted in showing their relations to "reality," or the abstract being that was God's mind. Medieval bestiaries abounded in illustrated accounts of animals that were viewed as reenacting episodes from the Old and New Testaments, such as Christ's martyrdom. Beavers, whales, and eagles duplicated in their lives, it was believed, the events of the Christian drama.

Sense data, moreover, or what the five senses collected from the physical world, were viewed with profound suspicion. Not only were the five senses understood as generally unreliable, but they were also seen as deceptive, seductive of reason, and likely to lead the observer away from what was "real" or "true." "Reality," again, was the abstract mind, or *verbum,* that had created everything, and it was by definition not physical. Because of this belief, other statements of Frederick were viewed as subversive, especially of recognized masters. "We discovered by hard-won experience," he wrote in *On the Art of Hunting with Birds,* "that the deductions of Aristotle, whom we followed when they appealed to our reason, were not entirely to be relied upon." In conversation, Frederick was reported to have said, "One should accept as truth only that which is proved by the force of reason and by nature." Pope Gregory IX correctly saw in these ideas a great danger, that of a society of men in which reason and experiment would take precedence over divine revelation. In fact, many questioned whether Frederick believed in God at all.

The rest of Frederick's behavior no doubt struck the Church, along with quite a few ordinary people, as equally disturbing. On the one hand, he understood the value of political theater as well as any ruler ever since. On the other, he reorganized politics on secular lines, thereby producing the first modern political state, with hints of democracy in some of its practices. The historian Jacob Burckhardt has described Frederick as the first emperor to turn the political state into a "work of art," but questions of beauty, mortal rather than religious, dominated all of his innovations.

Certainly his traveling royal theater, moving up and down Italy and across his favorite Kingdom of Two Sicilies, was meant to astonish, suggesting to the crowds that gathered wherever he went that one need not gain admission to heaven to catch sight of the miraculous, that it might be provided here and now, and even for the sinful, by an emperor who had already been compared with a flashing comet and who was regarded as an *immutator mirabilis,* a creator of the amazing. In addition to the masses of knights, mostly German and clad in bright steel, and the baggage train of armorers and saddle makers that would normally accompany someone of Frederick's growing power and legendary invincibility,

FIGURE 1. Hunting falcons with hoods. From *De arte venandi cum avibus,* by Frederick II.

he brought with him judges, administrators, a Saracen bodyguard, countless slaves, and Moorish officials. But this was only the beginning. His menagerie traveled with him: camels, caged and tethered hawks, horned owls and barn owls, peacocks, Syrian doves, Indian parakeets, African ostriches; and more: leopards, panthers, lions, apes, bears, a giraffe, and an elephant, the latter a gift from King John of Jerusalem, and carrying on its back a delicate tall tower; and still more: acrobats, magicians, rope dancers, and the famous dancing harem of Saracen women (dancing on rolling balls, beating tambourines), and the eunuchs who supervised them. The threat and delight were there for all to see, the declaration of independence, the announcement of the new importance of the individual soul and consciousness. Frederick's procession was a heavenly and earthly caravansary, a mingling of dreams, exotic visions, and splendors.

The emperor's threat became clearer, if that were necessary, in the laws that he drew up, with the assistance of the eloquent Pier della Vigna, for the administration of Sicily. These were collected in the so-called *Leges Augustales,* whose very title compared Frederick with the Roman emperor Augustus. Here Frederick chose to rely on ancient Roman, rather than religious, ideas of justice, and on administrators and judges who would be trained at his newly established University of Naples. Sicily, the new state, or "work of art," was to be run along strictly secular lines, with those in charge learned as much in the classics, and Roman law

modified to suit the new age, as in theology. The University of Naples in fact was set up as a deliberate challenge to the papal University of Bologna, which had schooled prelates in Church doctrine for over a century. The emperor offered full scholarships and cheap lodgings to students that he attracted from all over Italy. The *notari,* who were expected to write, dispute, show a thorough legal knowledge, understand the finer points of philosophy (including Platonic philosophy), and transcribe the government's masses of documents and orders, were educated here. Among its visitors, after its founding in 1224, was surely Giacomo da Lentino.

Little is known of Giacomo's life. He survives in his poetry and in the single most significant innovation in literature in the past eight hundred years, his invention of the sonnet, with all that it came to mean for human expression. Born in 1188, six years earlier than Frederick, he died in 1240, or ten years before Frederick's paradoxically pious death in 1250, when he insisted on dressing himself in the robes of a penitent, receiving the last rites, and making his confession. The two men knew and probably liked

FIGURE 2. Hooding the falcon; training; riding to the hunt. From *De arte venandi cum avibus,* by Frederick II.

each other. This much can be deduced from their professional and literary relations. That they were acquainted with each other, and even very well, is made plain from Frederick's *leges,* which placed the appointment of court *notari* directly in his hands, an unusual step and one intended to guarantee promotion by merit. There were just fourteen *notari* in all of Frederick's Sicilian kingdoms, a fact suggestive of Giacomo's importance and of his intimate relations with the emperor.

Frederick complimented his *notaro* most, of course, by imitating him in writing sonnets, a detail also indicative of their intimacy. Other members of Frederick's entourage did the same. Pier della Vigna, Frederick's most trusted confidant until his exposure as a traitor and his suicide in 1249, wrote sonnets (one is included in the selections that follow in Part II), as did Rinaldo d'Aquino, Jacopo Mostacci, L'Abate di Tiboli, Mazzeo di Ricco da Messina, Filippo da Messina, Bondie Dietaiuti, Maestro Francesco, Megliore degli Abati, Maestro Torrigiano, Pucciandone Martelli, and Ugo di Massa. Some fifty-eight sonnets survive of the poets of the *scuola siciliana* that developed around Frederick. Of these, twenty-six are definitely by Giacomo da Lentino. Three more are of doubtful authenticity.

But where the facts of Giacomo's life are absent, the flavor of his time—the spirit of the poets around him and of Frederick's

personality—may suffice to explain a good deal about him and his inventiveness. The first thing to be noted is that it was clearly a methods of irrigation and livestock breeding, and encouraged time of great expansion and originality, in Frederick's Italy at least, a time appreciative of changes. This was as true in architecture and mathematics as in science and literature. Frederick built more than twenty big castles in his "dear" province of Apulia alone, among them that of Lucera, whose massy walls could contain up to ten-thousand troops. Throughout his sprawling empire, whose power and elegance he expected to match those of ancient Rome, he constructed over sixty major fortresses, as well as grand hunting castles. At Capua, he helped in the design of the castle towers, which survive, and it is plausible that he participated in designs elsewhere. Like many at his court, he delighted in mathe-

FIGURE 3. Feeding the falcon; four steps in tethering the falcon, showing the proper tethering knot. From *De arte venandi cum avibus,* by Frederick II.

matics and mathematical puzzles. He experimented with novel efforts to discover the "earliest common language of mankind," at one point ordering a group of children to be brought up without exposure to any language, in the vain hope of learning what sort of speech they might arrive at by themselves (none, apparently). Frederick also established a system for licensing medical doctors, and permitted the dissection of corpses for anatomical studies. Many of these sound accomplishments and modern approaches to problems were to be obliterated, in some cases for a century or two, in the ecclesiastical waves of reaction that swept Europe after his death and the death of his son, King Manfred, a short while later. But for a brief period his comet shone, and its light flashed into obscure corners.

What also needs to be noted is that while Frederick favored change or originality, he seems never to have favored change for its own sake, or indiscriminately. Reason, experiment for the sake of new knowledge about the world, a love of beauty, and a desire to recapture and "make modern" the past guided him in everything. There was, especially, no flippant dismissal of past thinkers in his actions, only a rather typical medieval desire to assimilate them, where possible, to what he saw as the freshly evolving present. This could be seen in his treatment of Aristotle, who was to be challenged where he was wrong but whose ideas about classifying birds according to species, for instance, Frederick

willingly accepted. It carried over as well into the educational
system at Naples, which retained the traditional medieval *trivium*
in place at the University of Bologna, but with important new
embellishments. Giacomo had certainly been schooled in what was
called the *trivium,* or three chief medieval subjects, *grammatica,
rhetorica,* and *dialecta. Grammatica* meant the study of Latin ex-
clusively, and by that was also conventionally meant catechistical
uses of Church Latin. Did students at the emperor's new university
also study classical Roman literature? The question cannot be
answered with certainty, but it is worth noting that Frederick's
court was full of translators and investigators of ancient texts,
from Arabic and Greek as well as Latin, and that the study of
Roman law was deemed essential. *Rhetorica,* the most highly es-
teemed of medieval subjects, meant logic, debate, writing, and
poetry—the latter considered the loftiest form of language and
necessarily inclusive of logic. Aristotle's *Logic* was certainly studied at Naples, and this despite Pope Innocent III's banning of all
study of Aristotle in the year 1205, presumably in fear of dangerous new applications. Students learning *rhetorica* were also trained
in copying texts, called *dictare;* certainly the *notari* would have
been. Interestingly, *dictare* came rapidly to be interchangeable
with *scrivere,* to write, and even to write creatively. The modern
German *dichten,* meaning to compose poetry, and derived from
dictare, is a survivor of this happy confusion. *Dialecta* referred to
the study of philosophy, and it is here that Frederick's students
most drastically departed from the usual concentration on theology. Plato's *Timaeus* had been translated into Latin in the early
decades of the thirteenth century. If not at Naples, then at Frederick's court itself, Giacomo must have come to know intimately
this most luminous of Plato's dialogues, with its pagan account of
the creation and its description of the exact organization of the
human soul and heaven. Indeed, one may imagine that the ratios[5]
presented in the *Timaeus* made so deep an impression on the still
young poet-lawyer-*notaro,* as they naturally would in his world of
new architecture and logic, that they sprang naturally to mind, in
the manner of inspiration, as he wrote the first sonnet, perhaps
between 1225 and 1230.

5. A detailed discussion of these ratios appears in Part III, pp. 189–90.

The form would instantly have struck him, one may imagine, as appropriate to the mind of his emperor. The sonnet combines past with present, while transforming both. It also makes possible a new type of writing—silent, introspective, deeply personal—whose tendencies were already to be seen in the performed lyrics of Walther von der Vogelweide and even in the epic *Parzival* by Wolfram von Eschenbach. In thus announcing a new individuality and self-consciousness in poetry, the sonnet form must have seemed ideally suited to an emperor, and an intellectual as well as a political community, Frederick's court and the students at his new university, passionately attracted to the frontiers of emotion and experience.

As to the past: the octave of the sonnet is an imitation of the *strambotto,* a type of Sicilian peasant song that Frederick and his companions would have recognized. It is likely that they would also have seen the sestet-inspiration, which Giacomo added to the octave, as philosophically and mathematically familiar. The sonnet's ratios—of 6 : 8 : 12—would have reminded them of the *Timaeus.*[6] If not, it is plausible that Giacomo would have explained what he had done: reproduced the architecture of the soul, even the architecture of the meditative mind of God, in words on a sheet of paper. He might have added that the new form was designed to bring its readers, and those who wrote in it, closer to understanding the biblical assertion that man had been made in

---

6. The sonnet has commonly been regarded as an arithmetical structure, in which six lines are added to eight lines to produce fourteen. As I show in Part III, pp. 187–90, this point of view is incorrect. The sonnet is in fact an architectural structure, in which the ratios, or proportions of the significant numbers, make up a design which is in effect three-dimensional, as is the case with rooms, or the architecture of heaven as Plato envisaged it. Thus the total number of lines, fourteen, is relatively unimportant to understanding the structure of the form. What matters is the relationship proportionally of the octave to the sestet, and to the twelve lines that they enclose. One result of this "enclosure" is the natural tendency of many sonnets to couplets in the final lines, even when they do not actually rhyme, and to the development of the Shakespearian couplet ending at a later date (see p. 188). Medieval authors were fascinated with the relations of architecture to poetry generally, however, as titles ranging from Saint Augustine's fifth-century *City of God* (*Civitas Dei*) to the fifteenth-century *Castle of Perseverance* attest.

the image of God, the silent mind-creator of everything, who was to be wooed with prayer, or words, or poetry.

Another sort of wooing would also have occurred to them. Those around Frederick, and the emperor himself, would surely have thought of the courtly love poetry of Provence and the *Minnesang* lyrics of Germany, which they not only knew but imitated. The secular uses of the sonnet, as a sort of epistle to be sent to a distant (or not so distant) woman—the sonnet's ideal design as a silent messenger of illicit love—would have endowed it with special appeal. If the love contents of their own sonnets are any indication, that is exactly what it had.

It is impossible to imagine, though, that Frederick and his poet-friends would not have been even more deeply interested in the two most novel features of Giacomo's new type of poem: its departure from the performed poetry of the day, and its treatment of emotions with logic. Still, they may not have marveled at his invention as much as we do. It was not unreasonable that a *notaro,* or lawyer, who was also a poet, working among silent legal documents, should produce a silent type of poem, and still less unlikely that one who had probably read classical Roman lyric poetry, and Plato, a poet despite himself, should think about writing meditative verse, and then do so. It was also not surprising to find such a poet-lawyer fascinated with the relations of logic and poetry. What was truly unexpected was that he saw logic as a method that might reach beyond the usual—an arrangement of clauses, a statement of a problem, *rhetorica*—into a resolution of emotional problems. This perhaps led him to the next step. If an emotional problem were to be resolved within a mere fourteen lines, and in isolation, it would have to be resolved in a particular way: by the poet and the poem themselves, and within the mind of the poet. There was no one else, no outside, no audience. It was in perceiving this, and then creating a poetry to match, that Giacomo arrived at a stroke of genius that was to lead to major changes in how most poets and other writers were to write ever since.

One of the first effects of Giacomo's discovery was a change in attitudes toward words and reading. The well known anecdote about Saint Ambrose reading silently in his cell, as early as the fourth century, and astonishing his fellow monks, who were accustomed only to hearing words read aloud with lips moving, illustrates the pervasive conviction that all written language was somehow meant to be performed, even in private. The anecdote, recounted by Saint Augustine in his *Confessions,* illustrates too an early medieval fascination with silent reading. Hundreds of years old by the time Giacomo wrote his first sonnet, the story anticipates a time when masses of men and women would begin to read and write silently and alone, and to confront their values in a new literature of the self.

The First Hundred Years,
and Later Influences

The invention of the sonnet did not, of course, "create" self-sciousness. Appearing as it did at the court of Frederick II, it led to a fashion in self-conscious, silent, and meditative literature that continues into our own day. It led to a fashion in a new sort of imaginative literature as well, the literature in which concrete images would replace allegorical personifications, thereby promoting a new method of symbolism with more direct and clear connections to the subconscious. Chrétien de Troyes and the courtly love poets of Provence had similarly created a fashion for courtly love literature. But as Maurice Valency has pointed out in his study of the courtly love lyric, *In Praise of Love* (New York, 1958), courtly love poetry certainly did not create courtly love; it provided a form, and a mirror, in which to see more clearly what was probably commonplace. What now remains is some analysis of the new silent fashion.

It is surely obvious, though it needs mentioning, that the requirements of poetry meant to be set to music and sung, as opposed to poetry meant for silent reading, or reading aloud, differ so greatly as to produce, almost automatically, very different writing. Song is generally intolerant of complex imagery, though it thrives on simple plot and repetition. This is due as much to the music as to the nature of performance. Usually, in fact, two or more types of music must be absorbed at once, that of the players and voices, and that of the lyrics, with their ideas. Since sound always matters most in a musical performance—its very condition is aural—any complex images are bound to create a distraction, an imbalance between music and words, and ultimately confusion. If complex images come up in performed songs, they must probably be repeated fairly often, as in a refrain, to achieve clarity and balance

with the music. The richness of performed songs lies in the performance, not—or seldom—in the lyrics themselves.

Just the opposite is the case with the richness of imaginative
poetry, or meditative lyrics meant to be read in private or at most
to a few people. This is probably due as much to the handling of
time as to the inward-turning nature of personal silence. In performance, time is fleeting. It passes without pause. The audience must
surrender a good deal of its capacity for reflection. In privacy and
silence, however, readers may grant themselves total control, stop-
ping and starting at will, concentrating on a particular phrase,
repeating their readings of hard passages, reading sections and
words at random, rearranging a text in their minds, allowing asso-
ciations with past experiences and other texts to suggest themselves, and more of these than could possibly be managed during
a public reading or performance. The poet aware of these flexibili-
ties, really a flexibility of time, as was Giacomo, and his successors
in sonneteering, has a unique opportunity. He can focus on the
particular, the unusual, the concrete, the purely intellectual, exploring implications that would bewilder an audience listening to
instrumental music and singing. He can also create lengthy complex comparisons, or conceits, with twists, turns, and resolutions
incomprehensible to the hurried attention of a public audience
also listening to music.

Giacomo's sonnets overflow with concrete images and conceits.
In sonnet IX, for instance, he compares the withering of a cut lily
to his own internal "fasting" and "fading," cut off from the woman
he loves. In the second quatrain, his refined love, unknown to
hearts of a "weaker nature," is seen as an eagle that "swoops" and
"ravages" by "nature." The theme throughout is nature, what is
natural, for lilies, eagles, and the poet himself. Oddly, what is
natural for him, he announces, is his self-tormenting "fate" of
serving and adoring, or praising, his Lady as "best," no matter what
she does. The idea that a love that ravages him has become as
natural for him as it is for a lily to be joined to its stem is pur-
sued into the sestet. Here, by implication, the poet pleads with his
Lady to keep him from loving others. Were he to do so, he would
become "unnatural," so he feels. She can rescue him by accepting
him. His heart, he declares, can never part from her. Yet the focus
is less on her acceptance than on the destructive eagle of his love,

of which he has had "knowledge" since he first glimpsed her. By implication, too, this love is a sort of "natural disease," an idea common enough among courtly love poets (Giacomo takes up this issue more explicitly in sonnet XI).

The image of glass in sonnet X is similarly complex, with its play on glass and mirrors, on the fragility of both, and on their ability—despite how easily they may be shattered—to allow sunlight to pass through them or reflect off them harmlessly. This poem is about light and love. Each is seen as a force, and alters or "defaces" whatever it pierces and wherever it "reflects." Each, therefore, in some sense causes invisible "pain." In the sestet, the ideas of light and love are combined into a new image, that of fire, the fire of two lovers, which can become "visible," so that both lovers can see it, only if they get together. The poem is less a plea for this, though, than a careful and "shrewd" image itself, of the process of falling in love, or of being pierced by intense emotional "light."

It is the concreteness and complexity of the images that is interesting here, not the images themselves, which are conventional. The novel handling of the ordinary is what matters. Giacomo manages a change both small and momentous, especially when one considers where it would lead. Any reader familiar with the poets of Provence, or with lyrics of their northern French trouvère imitators, will surely notice a shift in emphasis in these two sonnets, a shift away, slightly but significantly, from images vaguely suggested and then abandoned to images offered with greater physical weight, because they are more detailed, and lengthier, and because they seem to carry all by themselves the major feelings of the poems. The lily and eagle of sonnet IX and the glass and fire of sonnet X have become symbols in the modern sense of becoming gateways to internal conflicts.

At the same time—another shift in emphasis—the persona of performed songs vanishes. It is replaced by a person, or at least a totally personal note. Both issues need some explanation.

A persona is an invented being designed as a deliberate replacement for the author, or as a mask. The presence of such an invention is always indicated, either by an announcement (as at the beginning of Dostoievsky's *Notes from Underground* or T. S. Eliot's "The Love Song of J. Alfred Prufrock") or by certain techniques, or both. Often, and especially in popular love songs, a blurring takes place, so that the song appears to be personal when in fact it is—if not personal—simply universal, sung in a way by a "personification," the performer. This occurs because of the audience's temptation to confuse the performer with his lyrics. The temptation is heightened if the performer is also the author of the lyrics. Nevertheless, the truly personal may be absent, as a brief reference to a more recent popular love song may easily demonstrate.

The first stanza of the popular "A Bicycle Built for Two" presents a typical performer-persona, who addresses not a specific "lady" but any lady, and more than her, any listening audience, anonymous and hopeful of success in love:

> Daisy, Daisy, give me your answer, do!
> I'm half crazy over the love of you!
> It won't be a stylish marriage—
> We can't afford a carriage,
> But you'll look sweet
> On the seat
> Of a bicycle built for two.

The jollity of these lines is achieved by a stock name, catch phrases, and the form. "Daisy" is never described. The name is a typical selection from the many female names-after-flowers. It can scarcely refer to an actual person. "Half crazy," a phrase whose sophistication and lightness result from the adverb "half," is a watered-down nineteenth-century version of the courtly love sentiment of adoration. The lines are clearly social rather than private, with references to public acts of obeisance—mirroring the idea of service to the beloved in Provençal courtly love poetry—and public ceremonies (riding to a wedding on a bicycle built for two) and a public problem (a lack of money). Importantly, the writing itself, with its lines of varying length, shows an adaptation to a melody, or performance. The actual feelings of the lover in love with Daisy, and Daisy herself, never (one might almost whisper, Thank God) show up here. If they did, the audience might feel something other than good cheer: a gloomy sympathy.

It is precisely this performer-persona that Giacomo eliminates, with the result that the truly personal, together with its genuine conflicts, makes an appearance. This is not to suggest that another persona, a lover-persona blended with a poet-persona, is not present in Giacomo's sonnets, only that the performer-persona, concerned with audience reactions, music, simplicity of imagery, and generalized emotions expressed in catch phrases, has vanished.

What is the personal? Certain key points can perhaps be made about this admittedly difficult term. Clearly, it must be distinguished from the merely obscure, on the one hand, and a tormenting of language, a twisting of syntax into freakishness, on the other. Private references, to names and facts important to the poet but to no one else, cannot make for personal poetry, only for obscurity in need of explanation. A twisting of the language, or the use of jargon, amounts in the end to a mere nervous avoidance of clichés—another form of obscurity—not a confrontation with inner conflict. As a result, freakish usages and jargon can usually be reduced to what is hackneyed, when the "camouflage" is stripped away, while clichés in themselves clearly reveal nothing personal, only a desperate desire to please at any cost. This is perhaps what the critic R. P. Blackmur had in mind when he took to task much of the poetry of e. e. cummings on the grounds that when its odd syntax and peculiar word combinations were deciphered, only quite ordinary and trite ideas remained. This may also be why *vers libre* is so difficult to write, what Robert Frost called "playing tennis without a net." Freedom, if it is not simply an illusion, at least in its pure sense, may in most cases simply be an invitation to self-indulgence, rather than its opposite, a moving self-consciousness.

There is, in the best personal poetry, a deep paradox involved, which may become visible at this point. It is that the personal, or the thrill of the mind revealed for all to see, in all of its individual intensity, may be possible only when the methods of the poetry are impersonal. The greatest intimacy may emerge from the greatest artifice and the greatest privacy, as at a secret meeting of secret lovers. Frustration, in the mind of a gifted artist, can produce revelation, but most often in a poetry that submits to the strictness of a chosen form, rather than simply to the desires and views of the poet, and which yet remains vivid and conversational language. This is not to suggest that "free verse," or (really) irregular verse, cannot be personal, only that it probably becomes most personal at those moments when it verges on the formal or becomes regu-

lar, while still ambient with passion and life, as in the regular ca-
dences of Whitman or Blake. In a perfectly traditional manner, a
frustrated conflict between form and feeling can thus evoke a dis-
arming openness of spirit, and personal revelation. But the revelation comes about through another sort of frustration as well,
through the frustration and reconciliation of powerful contradictory passions. Here it is not a question of "she loves me, she loves
me not" but of "I love her, I love her not," a taxing conflict of the
poet's own desires. The personal poem, or any truly personal piece
of writing, in fact may be said to begin with deep contradictions,
with passions and ideas that oppose and refute each other, and
that yet exist simultaneously, and with all of the frustration and
growing self-awareness that accompany this familiar type of suffering, the stuff of life itself, as the poet struggles for meaning.
"My love is as a fever, longing still / For that which longer nurseth
the disease, / Feeding on that which doth preserve the ill, / Th'
uncertain sickly appetite to please"—the Shakespearian contradiction, in sonnet 147, of longing for the same "sick" love that one
would wish destroyed, or of enjoying how this feverish appetite
"feeds" on what increases one's despair, or "ill," is a formula for
countless personal poems, or for personal honesty. Beyond this, it
may be observed that any satisfying meaning for this sort of struggle must be found in the poem itself, or in the poet and his poem,
not in the outside world. The poem is the locus of reconciliation of
opposed passions. In successful sonnets, the reconciliation takes
place in the sestet. Often the reconciliation involves a change of attitude or even character—in other words, courage—as when in his
sonnet XI Giacomo looks to his "spirit" to "guide" him, because
his Lady will not or cannot. The process is perhaps what Yeats
was thinking of when he said that when he revised his poems he
revised himself. Certainly Oedipus finds that the "fault" lies in
himself, not simply in his stars. Hamlet remains as baffling and
controversial as he is "true to life," becomes the most fascinating
of dramatic characters, because of his contradictions: he loves and
hates, he decides and hesitates, he goes mad and becomes sane, he
dismisses and praises, he jeers and craves, he hopes and surrenders—and all of these at once, and while also concentrating on
changing himself even as he assumes responsibility for his frightening situation of regicide. Feelings in contradiction, feelings mu-

tually exclusive yet held in a single heart, a heart that is torn as it
seeks to resolve them into an elusive harmony, are what produce
the amazing personal signature of the best writers.

In Giacomo's earliest sonnets, and in most of the best of his
contemporaries and successors, these contradictory emotions are
present, even as in most courtly love poetry they are not. Sonnet XI, for instance, paints a vivid struggle between the desires of
the poet-lover to conceal and reveal his pain in love. The struggle
produces a new pain, of comparison with other lovers who have
no trouble hiding their "love-disease." At the same time, there is
no hint that the double-pain felt by the poet-lover is to be exhibited to a public not directly concerned. There are no stock
names applied to some ghostly Lady's image, no catch phrases,
no performer-persona. The double-pain is instead meant to be
exhibited to the form of the poem itself, and in the poem, and for
the benefit of the resolution achieved in the strong, delicate sestet.
Here, in a quiet whisper of joy, the poet discovers how his own
spirit may shepherd him, allowing him to deserve to live among
people, as he feels he "should."

A comparison with Provençal courtly love poetry reveals just
the reverse of this, and nearly all the time, and illuminates the
new direction that Giacomo was staking out for the sonnet. In the
famous *canzone* beginning "Quant l'aura doussa s'marzis" of Cercamon, a bitter despair, striking in itself even as it is conventional,
expresses perfectly the courtly love poet's practiced wooing:

> Quant l'aura doussa s'marzis
> e·l fuelha chai de sul verjan
> e l'auzelh chanjon lor latis,
> et ieu de sai sospir e chan
> d'Amor que·m te lassat e pres,
> qu'ieu encar no l'aic en poder.
>
> Las! qu'ieu d'Amor non ai conquis
> mas las trebalhas e l'afan,
> ni res tant greu no·s covertis
> com so que·m plus vau deziran;
> ni tal enveja no·m fai res
> cum fai so qu'ieu non posc aver.
>   (BASE MS.: C.)

[When the sweet wind goes sour
And the leaf lets go its bough,
And the birds' voices cower,
Then I know how to sing and sigh
For Love, Love's prison-power,
Power I never could beat.

My misery never savored
Any trophy of love but a blow.
There's nothing for me so ill-favored
As the woman I most crave to know.
My desire in pain never wavered
From the thing that I simply can't get.]

Cercamon's verses limn his despair with a warm, almost tropical enthusiasm. At the same time, the mood is urbane, autumnal. This careful mixture of attitudes nearly conceals the singleness of the emotion. There is only longing here, no doubt about its value or motives. The performer-persona grieves, but only as one who must "sing and sigh" with an ironic self-pity, in coincidence with the change of seasons from summer to fall. Nor should saying this diminish the beauty of the lines, or their artistic mastery, which is smoothed with an ornate and glossy loveliness of a type often found in Provençal courtly love poetry. But it does indicate a decisive limitation. A single emotion, whether of longing or despair or devotion, and no matter how powerfully expressed, cannot by itself reveal the complexities of character, or the hard battle for self-honesty. At best, single emotions create stereotypes, or performer-personae, facades, often interesting, sometimes marvelous, meant to entertain and soothe. Their purpose, as is clear in many an adventure story, is to reduce the portrait of character to a silhouette, so that the focus may fall on a single type of action, on violence in the adventure story, on service in the courtly love poem. The mood is uncomplicated by questions of values. The values, between poet and audience, are understood and not to be questioned.

Giacomo's newly invented "silent" sonnets were meant to push beyond this, thereby fulfilling a tendency already apparent, to some extent in the long narratives of Chrétien de Troyes, in France, but more impressively in the Germanic poetry of the north. Some of the finest lyrics of Walther von der Vogelweide, and Wolfram's epic *Parzival,* introduce self-conscious and meditative moments and scenes, although the more familiar performer-persona still dominates and simplifies characterization. Hints and even convictions that accepted values and views of human nature needed to be challenged, in the work of these poets, as well as in the *Tristan und Isolde* of Gottfried von Strassburg, no doubt caught the receptive ear of Frederick II on his travels through his German kingdoms. There he would certainly have heard this quite remarkable poetry, and there his courtier-*notaro* Giacomo might have heard it too. The half-pagan spirit of the Germanic kingdoms remained half-defiant and questioning almost by nature, inclined to introspection. The ancient Teutonic forest gods and goddesses still called out, in folksongs and fate-governed epics such as the *Nibelungenlied,* to dark and triumphant passions in the souls of thousands of knights and their ladies, in voices full of clever magic, in the hundreds of castles linked as in a chain of civilization and soldiery from Salzburg to Aachen. Once the tendency toward meditative poetry had combined with silent literature, in Giacomo's sonnet, and once a fashion for this new type of literature had caught on at Frederick's court in Apulia, the only questions were what would be done with it and where it would lead.

It led to Dante, within a few brief decades. It led to the precise, intimate light of Dante's metaphors, earthy comparisons rendering the miraculous mundane and the mundane miraculous. It led eventually to Shakespeare. It led, still later, to Donne's beaten gold and his amazing image of a compass, whose legs, in "A Valediction: Forbidding Mourning," leaning and turning measure his heart's yearning for his wife. It led to the angelic lights of the images of Milton's *Paradise Lost,* with their caressing power, the power of soft storms, burning the last dark from heaven even as they sterilize the sepulchral dust of hell, burning hell's filth clean, so that anyone can see for himself the poisonous morbidity of excess, and see it with a perfect clarity never before known. It led or contributed, in fact, to all of the splendid variety of the modern literary experience.

In Dante's *Commedia* one encounters an encyclopedia of intimacy. For the first time, the poet is himself the central figure in a major literary work, one of the most sublime in the history of written language. In his political treatise *De monarchia,* Dante had already described the goal of civilization as the perfection of the human mind. He argued that this goal was most likely to be achieved not by a politically powerful pope but by a monarch schooled in justice and devoted to reason, who would minister to the secular lives of men even as the pope ministered to their religious ones. This was the political doctrine of Frederick II. It had been set down by the emperor in a letter to the Roman cardinals in 1239, in which he spoke of God as having "placed two lights in the firmament," that of the pope and that of the monarch. Its clear influence on Dante indicates the extent to which the greatest of Italian poets had accepted Frederick's model as his ideal. More significantly, Dante's vernacular poetry, and his defense of vernacular Italian, and specifically Sicilian, literature, in his *De vulgari eloquentia* (bk. I, ch. XII), shows his indebtedness to the vernacular poetry of Frederick's courtiers and the emperor himself:

> The Sicilian vernacular appears to arrogate to itself a greater renown than the others, both because whatever poetry the Italians write is called Sicilian, and because we find that very many natives of Sicily have written weighty poetry. . . . But those illustrious heroes Frederick Caesar and his happy-born son Manfred, displaying the nobility and righteousness of their character, as long as fortune remained favorable, followed what is human, disdaining what is bestial; wherefore those who were of noble heart and endowed with graces strove to attach themselves to the majesty of such great princes; so that in their time, whatever the best Italians first attempted first appeared at the court of these mighty sovereigns.[7]

Dante was to pay homage to Giacomo da Lentino in his *Purgatorio,* where he refers to Giacomo as one who, despite real achievement, did not attain to Dante's own *dolce stil nuovo* ("sweet new style"). But the greatest homage is offered by implication, in Dante's *La vita nuova,* which does not mention Giacomo. The book is Dante's love-autobiography, a series of sonnets interlaced with prose analyses of their structures and meanings. Dante here speaks of the sonnet as "showing forth my inward speech," a phrase neatly descriptive of the personal, silent quality, the meditative sweetness, of the new sort of literature.

---

7. *A Translation of the Latin Works of Dante Alighieri,* trans. A. G. Ferrers Howell (London, 1904), pp. 38–39.

In the *Commedia,* the grandest possible stage, a cosmic one stretching from hell to heaven, from confusion to certainty, from depravity to celestial glory, becomes the setting for personal discoveries. The daring of this is inconceivable without the groundwork of Giacomo's Sicilian sonnet. The *Commedia* is the first silent epic. In fact, it is the first major piece of silent literature in modern times. Its meditational qualities, the complexity of its conceits or comparisons, and the difficulties of its philosophical and scientific outlooks become the delicious acceptable joys of the reader who reads alone, the new reader of poetry. They are no more within the province of an audience listening to music and singing than would be the novels of Dostoievsky or Proust. This is not to say that the *Commedia* cannot be read aloud or even in part performed. But Dante's epic, written in exile, and focusing on personal-spiritual growth, and on a spiritual-intellectual vision, is designed for visionary and private readers. Erich Auerbach has pointed out how this intention meant a search for a new audience as well, an audience not necessarily of the noble classes but interested in poetry, and sharing the poet's concern with what poetry could accomplish at its imaginative and intimate best:

> The apostrophes to the reader [of the *Commedia*] are almost all couched in the imperative; none contains a plea for favor or indulgence, and nowhere does Dante speak like an author who looks upon his readers as customers. When Dante expresses his hope of favor and fame, he seems to be addressing posterity; and when he confesses his insufficiency, he is not pleading for indulgence but only explaining the superhuman dimensions of his task.[8]

The performer-persona, still present in Wolfram's *Parzival,* has clearly vanished. In implying this change, Auerbach points inadvertently to yet another result of the invention of the sonnet and its influence. This is the creation of a new and specifically modern literary tradition of great importance in the history of poetry since Dante, that of writing poetry for a literary-minded audience rather than simply for "customers," or members of the aristocracy. Dante takes as his standard the finest achievements of the best poets of the past, and looks to the best poets to come, to posterity, viewing

8. Erich Auerbach, *Literary Language and Its Public in Late Latin Antiquity and in the Middle Ages* (New York, 1965), p. 301.

them as masters, who, along with like-minded readers, will fully comprehend his efforts and success. Virgil is Dante's guide through much of the *Commedia*. The most ambitious of Roman poets, the author of the *Aeneid,* referred to as a "fountain of rich speech" and as "a glory and light of other poets," whose work Dante has zealously studied, is a paragon for this audience, together with readers, of whatever background or class, or era not yet begun, who worship the perfections of poetry.

This is a very different thing from writing for the aristocratic and emotional elite, those among the nobility in Provence whom the troubadours often referred to as the "elect" because they appreciated the noblest sort of love, or *fin amour.* It is also very different from simply basing one's poetry on biblical texts alone, or earlier texts of other sorts, to conform with medieval notions of "truth," texts that seemed closer to the mind of God simply because they were old. Dante writes for what he calls the *cor gentile,* the well bred and even educated heart or spirit, of all classes. He writes nearly as much for the sake of poetry as for the sake of God. His best successors over the centuries were often to write for the sake of poetry only, or for the sake of the deepest self-contradictory emotions, or in the hope of emulating the best poets of the past, Dante among them.

In undertaking to change the very audience for poetry, and to seriously alter the nature of literary tradition, Dante seems to owe much to the invention of the sonnet. From the start, Giacomo and his contemporaries at Frederick's court had seen the sonnet as an epistolary spark for dialogue between poets, deeply conscious of the form as capable of a new literary intimacy. Giacomo exchanges sonnets, in dialogue form, with L'Abate di Tiboli. Jacopo Mostacci does the same with Pier della Vigna. Giacomo's sonnet *Amor è un desio che ven da core* (see pp. 62–63) becomes the third voice in a *tenzone,* or debate, between Mostacci and della Vigna.[9] The practice continued and expanded among the poets of the *dolce stil nuovo.* Sending sonnets back and forth, Dante participated in a new form of literary correspondence, with Brunetto Latini, Cino da Pistoia, and Guido Cavalcanti. Other poets, such

9. Impersonal varieties of the *tenzone* were known in Italy, having originated among the twelfth-century troubadour poets of Provence, who debated abstract issues in *chanson* form.

as Folgore da San Gimignano, had already extended the range of subjects that the sonnet might easily handle, beyond the familiar subject of secular love. Folgore's sequence of twelve sonnets, on the months of the year, and his sequence of seven, on the days of the week, demonstrated in splendidly developed concrete images that the personal and meditative could combine powerfully with description. A fashion for the new sort of writing was in the air, and it was a natural, if tortuous, step beyond what others were doing to Dante's *Commedia,* with its combinations of intimacy, concreteness, and the broadest possible philosophy and spiritual devotion. Equally natural, in view of the new type of poetry, was Dante's transformation of the epic form itself. Virgil may be Dante's guide and master through much of the *Commedia,* but Dante's celebration of beauty on all possible levels is not the *Aeneid.* Nor is it the *Odyssey* (Dante had read Homer in poor Latin translations). In his essay "Dante and the Martial Epic," Robert Hollander has shown how Dante adapted the themes and techniques of these classical epics to his new Christian epic, turning the struggles of heroes into the pilgrimage of an ordinary man to the sight of God.[10]

The spread of the sonnet into all cultures speaking Western languages over the next few centuries, its continuing vitality in the present century, its sharp alive challenge to all those in the West who imagine themselves to be poets—all these facts, despite their importance, belie and even obscure the form's real significance, which may now be clearer. As writers began to create self-conscious characters and to produce literature meant to be read in silence, many of them influenced by Giacomo indirectly, through Dante and Petrarch and Boccaccio, the roles of the sonnet and its creator were largely forgotten, if in fact they were ever solidly understood. But the miracle and the evidence of it remained. As always in the history of literature, and the history of science too, it was the miracle of a single person, a single amazing mind, deeply influenced and aided by other amazing minds, and their pains and sorrows and innovations, but achieving something fresh and reaching adventurously beyond them, through passion and a gift, on its

10. Paper delivered at the annual meeting of the Dante Society of America, held at the Modern Language Association Convention in New York, December 1986.

own. Frederick's theatrical, scientific intelligence had attacked a corrupt politics and sought to overthrow an incorrect system of beliefs about the world. His courtier-*notaro* Giacomo all unwittingly helped to change how human beings were to look at themselves and express themselves, by bringing into their literature the great new facts of silence, introspection, and self-consciousness, by creating the lyric of the private soul.

II

Sonnets in the European Tradition

A Note on the Translations

The poems that follow have been selected for a variety of reasons. Most are from Italian and German, with a few from French and Spanish. The sonnet has been strongest in Italy and the German-speaking countries, with large numbers of extremely good ones produced in those cultures, which also contributed so much to its very nature: the invention and early development of the form in Italy, and the introspective aspect, incorporated from Germany and Austria. Excellent individual sonnets have been written in France and Spain as well, but many of these have been quite splendidly translated by others and are well known, especially those of Baudelaire. It seemed superfluous to repeat what could not be matched or improved.

A number of sonnets from Italian have been selected because they are both beautiful and crucial to understanding a form that has influenced Western culture so deeply. Quite a few appear here because they have not done so elsewhere, or because their earlier versions are archaic and creaky to modern tastes. Few translations outlast their makers or generations, and the art is as short-lived as roses or butterflies. A translator, especially of poetry, rarely grasps the many dimensions of his original. He may grasp one or several, usually those that match his own tastes, and those of his time and people, but only seldom, and probably without knowing that he has done so, can he lay aside his whims and prejudices long enough to allow the full complexity of another author's vision, and a foreign author's at that, to shine through into the new language. Baudelaire's translations of Poe are a famous exception. Dryden is peerless in his renderings of Horace. It is fashionable today to dismiss Pope's *Iliad* and *Odyssey*. Samuel Johnson, who knew less Greek than Shakespeare, preferred Pope to Homer, and for once that eclectic judge, as biased in his tastes as he was delightful in conversation, was not entirely wrong. Pope's English

43

catches the poetry and power and sweep of Homer better than any of his successors, in a wonderful matching of sensibilities, no doubt because he is so fine a poet, so great a master of English, in his own right. Rossetti's translations of many of the early Italian poets remain—to my mind—superb examples of the translator's art, and should be studied by readers interested in translation and in the brilliant early variety of Italian literature. In our own day, there has been no shortage of expert and gifted translators of poetry too, who have solved in different ways the translator's perpetual problem of contradictory loyalties. The ideal, never attained as one might wish, is loyalty to literalness and to liveliness, to another time and to one's own, to an alien style and an appropriate new style, to an alien viewpoint and a sensible equivalent viewpoint, to the original techniques and to the right approximations, and above all to the languages involved, to both of them, and to the poems, both the old and the new, as poems, to their spirit as well as letter, to their power and richness as poetry. Despite nearly ten years of work, I am conscious of many failures, of the arbitrariness of paraphrase where necessary, of the need, or so it seemed, to eliminate obscurities here and there, one hopes at little cost. The happy trust remains that this bilingual presentation will enable readers to see the loveliness of the originals as well, and to discover in this historically oriented selection, ranging over a number of cultures, a lens through which to begin to look not only at the development of the sonnet but of modern literature itself. For the English-speaking reader, the additional opportunity may also present itself, of enjoying the vast riches of sonnet composition in English, along with much that is fine in English literature, in a rather new way.

Textual Note

Texts are listed in the Bibliography. In various Italian poems, accents may differ according to texts used. The text of sonnet XI, by Giacomo da Lentino, follows Langley (see Part III, pp. 182 and 188). The division of sonnets into separate quatrains and tercets— with Giacomo da Lentino, Frederick II, Dante, Petrarch, Cellini,

Boscán, Lope de Vega, and Machado—follows accepted scholarly and editorial practice. For a discussion of Giacomo da Lentino's view of the sonnet as a single, undivided stanza, see Part III, pp. 176–78.

ITALIAN SONNETS

Giacomo da Lentino (1188–1240)

Sonetto IX

Lo giglio quand'è colto tost'è passo
da poi la sua natura lui no è giunta,
ed io, dacunque son partuto un passo
da voi, mia donna, dolemi ogni giunta:

perché d'amare ogni amadore passo,
in tante alteze lo mio core giunta;
cosí mi fere Amor, lavunque passo,
com'aghila quand'a la caccia è giunta.

Oi lasso me, che nato fui in tal punto,
s'unque no amasse se non voi, Chiú-gente!
Questo saccio, madonna, da mia parte:

in prima che vi vidi ne fui punto,
serviivi ed inoraivi a tutta gente;
da voi, bella, lo mio core non parte.

Sonnet IX

Once cut, the lily fades, and very fast—
Once cheated, naturally, of its basic nature.
So I: deprived of you, I seem to fast
And fade with pains of every possible nature.

For love like mine secures itself, too fast,
To heights unknown to hearts of a weaker nature.
So too, my love impales me, far too fast,
An eagle swooping, ravaging by nature.

How hopeless I would be, born to this fate,
If I loved someone else—not you, the best!
This knowledge, Lady, is certain on my part:

At once, on seeing you, I knew my fate—
To serve and praise you everywhere as best.
From you, my love, my heart can never part.

Giacomo da Lentino

Sonetto X

Sí come il sol, che manda la sua spera
e passa per lo vetro e no lo parte,
e l'altro vetro che le donne spera,
che passa gli occhi e va da l'altra parte,

cosí l'Amore fere là ove spera
e mandavi lo dardo da sua parte:
fere in tal loco che l'omo non spera
e passa gli occhi e lo core diparte.

Lo dardo de l'Amore, là ove giunge,
da poi che dà feruta sí s'aprende
di foco, ch'arde dentro e fuor non pare;

e li due cori insemola li giunge:
de l'arte de l'Amore sí gli aprende,
e face l'uno e l'altro d'amor pare.

Sonnet X

Just as the sun can spear straight through the face
Of any glass and no one seems to mind,
And like the glass that spears a woman's face
Straight through her eyes and climbs into her mind—

Just so true love can manage to deface
Wherever it wishes, shooting time out of mind
The pang whose pain you feel you cannot face,
To send you, through your eyes, out of your mind.

The pain of love, precisely where you feel it,
And once the pain begins, transforms itself
To fire, shrewd and cold, that none can see.

But if the fire's doubled, by two who feel it,
The power of love once more transforms itself,
Inspiring both with love that both can see.

Giacomo da Lentino

Sonetto XI

Molti amadori la lor malatia
portano in core, che 'm vista nom pare;
ed io nom posso, sì celar la mia
ch' ella nom paia per lo mio penare;

però che son sotto altrui segnoria,
nè di meve non ò neiente a fare,
se non quanto madonna mia voria,
ch' ella mi pote morte e vita dare.

Su' è lo core, e suo sono tutto quanto,
e chi non à comsiglio da suo core,
non vive imfra la gente como deve.

Càd io nom sono mio nè più nè tanto,
se non quanto madonna è de mi fore,
ed un poco di spirito ch' è 'n meve.

Sonnet XI

So many lovers carry their love-disease
Inside their hearts, where it cannot be seen,
But I cannot conceal my fierce unease
So that it does not glimmer through my pain.

I'm under just one woman's haughty eye—
She neither stirs nor does a thing, in truth—
Unless my Lady makes me some reply,
Because she can pronounce my life and death.

My heart is hers, me too—all, all for her—
And he who fails to listen to his heart
Can't live with people, as he should, or share.

I suffer thus: am neither here nor there,
Unless my Lady guides me, though apart,
Unless my bit of spirit guides me, here.

Giacomo da Lentino

Sonetto XXII

Chi non avesse mai veduto foco
no crederia che cocere potesse,
anti li sembraría sollazo e gioco
lo so isprendore, quando lo vedesse.

Ma s'ello lo toccasse in alcun loco,
ben li sembrara che forte cocesse:
quello d'Amore m'ha toccato un poco;
molto me coce: Deo, che s'aprendesse!

Che s'aprendesse in voi, madonna mia,
che mi mostrate dar sollazo amando,
e voi mi date pur pen'e tormento!

Certo l'Amore fa gran villania,
che no distringe te, che vai gabando;
a me che servo non dà isbaldimento.

Sonnet XXII

The man who hasn't ever seen a fire
Doesn't imagine that it can ever burn.
Instead it seems to him a joy, a player,
As he observes its splendid twist and turn.

But if he touches it in any spot
It seems to burn all right, in a sudden switch:
The fire of love has touched my heart a bit
And burned me a lot—God, let this fire catch!

And let it catch in you, my special woman,
Who makes a show of sweetly loving me
And offers me the purest hell and pain.

Love surely commits the sort of crime called common,
Ignoring you, who stroll about so free.
To me, love's slave, love offers no bright gain.

Giacomo da Lentino

Sonetto XXVIII

Lo basalisco a lo specchio lucente
traggi a morire con isbaldimento;
lo cesne canta piú gioiosamente
quand'è piú presso a lo so finimento;

lo paon turba, quando è piú gaudente,
poi ch'a suoi piedi fa riguardamento;
l'augel fenise s'arde veramente
per ritornare in novo nascimento:

In tal nature eo sentom'abenuto,
ch'allegro vado a moro a le belleze
e 'nforzo il canto presso a lo fenire,

e stando gaio torno dismaruto,
e ardendo in foco invoco in allegreze
per voi, Piú-gente, a cui spero redire.

Sonnet XXVIII

The basilisk before a lucid mirror
Surrenders to death in joyful agony;
The swan keeps singing with a joyful horror
When overwhelmed by its mortality;

The peacock, at its height of brilliant plumes,
Shivers in horror on glancing at its feet;
The phoenix bird consumes itself in flames
Completely, to return, reborn, complete.

I feel myself becoming this type of creature—
Happy to meet my death before great beauty
And pushing my song to glory at its last turn,

And right in the midst of joy feeling pure torture—
And burning in flames, renewing my happy duty
To you—so fine—to whom I would return.

Jacopo Mostacci (at court of Frederick II ca. 1240)

Tenzone con Pier della Vigna e Giacomo da Lentino

Sollicitando un poco meo savere
e cum lui mi vogliendo delettare,
un dubio che me misi ad avere
a vui lo mando per determinare.

Onn'omo dize ch'Amor ha podere
e gli corazi distrenze ad amare,
ma eo no lo voglio consentere
però ch'Amore no parse ni pare.

Ben trova l'om una amorositate
la quale par che nassa de plazere,
e zo vol dire om che sia amore.

Eo no li sazzo altra qualitate:
ma zo che è da vui voglio odere,
però ven fazo sentenziatore.

Debate with Pier della Vigna
and Giacomo da Lentino

Searching for a bit of self-improvement
And wishing to delight myself as well,
I'm sending you a problem that's arisen
For you to solve, or not, as time will tell.

Everybody says that love's a force
And pushes hearts into the wildest love-careers,
But I find myself quite unable to say, "Of course!"—
Because love's neither visible nor appears.

Granted, man is amorously inclined,
A disposition born of purest pleasure,
And therefore wants to say that love exists.

I wouldn't grant it other gifts, of mind,
But want to hear what judgment you would render
So I can judge this question. It persists.

Pier della Vigna (d. 1249)

Però ch'Amore no se pò vedere
e no si tratta corporalemente,
manti ne son de sí folle sapere
che credono ch'Amor sia niente.

Ma po' ch'Amore si faze sentere
dentro dal cor signorezar la zente,
molto mazore presio de' avere
che se 'l vedessen vesibelemente.

Per la vertute de la calamita
como lo ferro atrai no se vede,
ma sí lo tira signorivelmente;

e questa cosa a credere me 'nvita
ch'Amore sia, e dame grande fede
che tuttor sia creduto fra la zente.

[Reply to Jacopo Mostacci]

Just because love cannot be seen at all
And doesn't appear as a corporeal thing,
A lot of people who don't know anything at all
Believe love must be absolutely nothing.

But since love makes itself most powerful
From inside the heart, as everybody's king,
It ought to be a lot more valuable
Than if it were a visible sort of thing.

You cannot see a magnet's powerful wave
When iron attracts it, yet you understand
Its power is irresistibly unfurled.

And this fact simply invites me to believe
That love exists, and lets me comprehend
That—always—it's obeyed throughout the world.

Giacomo da Lentino

Amor è un desio che ven da core
per abundanza de gran plazimento,
e gli ogli en prima generan l'amore
e lo core li dà nutrigamento.

Ben è alcuna fiata om amatore
senza vedere so 'namoramento,
ma quell'amor che strenze cum furore
da la vista di gli ogli ha nascimento:

ché gli ogli representan a lo core
d'onni cosa che veden bon' e rio,
cum'è formata naturalemente;

e lo cor, che di zo è concipitore,
imazina, e li plaze quel desio:
e questo amore regna fra la zente.

[Reply to Jacopo Mostacci and Pier della Vigna]

Love's a desire that sweeps out of the heart
From immensities of the grandest pleasure,
And your eyes ignite its visible start
And your heart supplies nutrition beyond all measure.

It's very fine to play the lover's part
Without a glimpse of any beloved creature,
But powerful love of the most passionate sort
Holds vistas born of a purely optical nature:

For your eyes create impressions on your heart
Of all the fine things that your eyes can capture
Exactly as their forms appear in nature,

And your heart, participating with its art,
Reflects on this, and infuses it with rapture:
And this love runs the whole world's natural order.

Federico II (1194–1250)

Sonetto

Misura, provedenza e meritanza
fa esser l'uomo savio e conoscente,
e ogni nobiltà buon senn'avanza
e ciascuna riccheza fa prudente.

Né di riccheze aver grande abundanza
faria l'omo ch'è vile esser valente,
ma della ordinata costumanza
discende gentileza fra la gente.

Omo ch'è posto in alto signoragio
e in riccheze abunda, tosto scende,
credendo fermo stare in signoria.

Unde non salti troppo omo ch'è sagio,
per grandi alteze che ventura prende,
ma tuttora mantegna cortesia.

Sonnet

Balance, providence and true refinement
Make any man both savvy and aware,
And every sort of grace means better judgment
And every sort of wealth produces care.

No mass of money, no matter how abounding,
Can make a coward a man of bravery.
Only habits of life with solid grounding
Can offer people true nobility.

The man placed in a lordly high position,
Who swims in money, falls hardest in the muck,
Believing his rank to be a solid fact.

That's why the wise won't jump beyond his station,
To greater heights presented him by luck,
But always keeps his tastefulness and tact.

Dante Alighieri (1265–1321)

Sonetto X

Tutti li miei penser parlan d'Amore;
e hanno in lor sì gran varietate,
ch'altro mi fa voler sua potestate,
altro folle ragiona il suo valore,

altro sperando m'apporta dolzore,
altro pianger mi fa spesse fiate;
e sol s'accordano in cherer pietate,
tremando di paura che è nel core.

Ond'io no so da qual matera prenda;
e vorrei dire, e non so ch'io mi dica:
così mi trovo in amorosa erranza!

E se con tutti voi fare accordanza,
convenemi chiamar la mia nemica,
madonna la Pietà, che mi difenda.

Sonnet X

My thoughts all speak unceasingly of love
And do so in a vast variety.
The one insists I want love's slavery,
The next that there's plain madness in the above,

The next, more hopeful, lets my joy improve,
The next, a frequent one, just makes me cry—
They just agree on wanting sympathy,
Trembling with what my heart is frightened of.

The outcome is I don't know what theme to take
And want to write and don't know what to say—
That's why I find myself in love's confusions!

And if I want real peace with all these passions
I'll have to ask my own worst enemy,
That Lady Pity, for help, for pity's sake.

Dante Alighieri

Sonetto XI

Con l'altre donne mia vista gabbate,
e non pensate, donna, onde si mova
ch'io vi rassembri sì figura nova
quando riguardo la vostra beltate.

Se lo saveste, non poria Pietate
tener più contra me l'usata prova,
chè Amor, quando sì presso a voi mi trova,
prende baldanza e tanta securtate,

che fere tra' miei spiriti paurosi,
e quale ancide, e qual pinge di fore,
sì che solo remane a veder vui:

ond'io mi cangio in figura d'altrui,
ma non sì ch'io non senta bene allore
li guai de li scacciati tormentosi.

Sonnet XI

With other women you jeer at how I look,
And never guess, my Lady, why I change,
Becoming someone who must look quite strange
When my two eyes take in your beauty's shock.

If you knew this, your pity could not take
Its usual tough line that makes me cringe.
The fact is, when love finds us at close range
It takes real heart and feels such solid luck

It lashes all my fears like ghosts demented,
And kills one here and banishes one there
Till love alone is left to look at you:

That's why I'm changed into a man askew,
Yet not so much that I can't roundly hear
My howling fears, now exiled and tormented.

Francesco Petrarca (1304–1374)

Rime sparse: 164

Or che 'l ciel e la terra e 'l vento tace
e le fere e gli augelli il sonno affrena,
notte il carro stellato in giro mena,
e nel suo letto il mar senz'onda giace,

vegghio, penso, ardo, piango; e chi mi sface
sempre m'è inanzi per mia dolce pena:
guerra è 'l mio stato, d'ira e di duol piena;
e sol di lei pensando ho qualche pace.

Così sol d'una chiara fonte viva
move 'l dolce e l'amaro, ond'io mi pasco;
una man sola mi risana e punge.

E perché 'l mio martìr non giunga a riva
mille volte il dì moro e mille nasco;
tanto da la salute mia son lunge.

Rime sparse: 164

Now that the sky and earth and wind are still
And sleep makes prisoners of birds and beasts,
Night runs her star-packed car through the round wastes
And the sea lies bedded down with not one swell—

I'm up, I think, I burn, I cry—so full
Is she in me, producing my sweet sweats.
My state of mind is war, full of rages, blasts
And only thinking of her provides a lull.

That's how a single source-spring, clear and spry,
Supplies the sweet and sour I feed upon.
One hand alone restores and stabs self-worth.

And making sure my pain won't ever die,
I die a thousand times and am reborn
Each day—so far I've come from my good health.

Francesco Petrarca

Rime sparse: 165

Come 'l candido pie' per l'erba fresca
i dolci passi onestamente move,
vertù che 'ntorno i fiori apra e rinove
de le tenere piante sue par ch'èsca.

Amor, che solo i cor leggiadri invesca
né degna di provar sua forza altrove,
da' begli occhi un piacer sì caldo piove,
ch'i non curo altro ben né bramo altr'ésca.

E co l'andar e col soave sguardo
s'accordan le dolcissime parole,
e l'atto mansueto, umile e tardo.

Di tai quattro faville, e non già sole,
nasce 'l gran foco, di ch'io vivo et ardo,
che son fatto un augel notturno al sole.

Rime sparse: 165

As her pure foot moves in her tender strolls
With white aloofness through the fresh green grass,
The force that opens flowers as her steps pass,
Refreshing them, seems pouring from her soles.

Love, pouring only through the finest souls
(Refusing to test its force in any worse place),
Rains from her lovely eyes with such warm grace
I crave no other bait, or fine details.

And with her walk and her most gentle glance
Her sweetest words roll in a single wave
With her most modest, slow advance.

From these four sparks, and not from them alone,
Bursts the great fire by which I burn and live,
And I've become a night bird in the sun.

Michelangelo Buonarroti (1475–1564)

Sonetto CXLVII

Giunto è già 'l corso della vita mia
Con tempestoso mar, per fragil barca
Al comun porto, ov'a render si varca
Conto e ragion d'ogni opra trista e pia.

Onde l'affettüosa fantasia,
Che l'arte mi fece idolo e monarca,
Conosco or ben com'era d'error carca,
E quel ch'a mal suo grado ogni uom desia.

Gli amorosi pensier, già vani e lieti,
Che fian or, s'a due morti m'avvicino?
D'una so 'l certo, e l'altra mi minaccia.

Né pinger né scolpir fia più che quieti
L'anima volta a quell'amor divino,
Ch'aperse a prender noi 'n croce le braccia.

Sonnet CXLVII

It's come already, the whole course of my life—
Through a stormy sea in a delicate open boat—
To the common harbor where everyone gets off
For account and judgment of all his bad and good.

I see now how my passionate ambition
That let me make an idol of my art,
And monarch of it too, was pure misprision,
The worst like that in every human heart.

Where's ambition now, so sassy, jealous,
Those lover's thoughts, as I face my double deaths,
The bodily death I'm sure of and my soul's loss?

Neither painting nor sculpture can leave my soul less zealous
For turning to God, His divinely loving truths,
Who spreads his arms to take us on His cross.

Benvenuto Cellini (1500–1571)

Ben molti si son messi a far sonetti

Ben molti si son messi a far sonetti,
e molti pochi son quei che fan bene;
ogni uom cognosce il ver da quel che viene,
chè le Muse ognun chiama; e pochi eletti.

Non val lo esprimer bene i sua concetti;
nè ben d'Amor mostrar suo galdio o pene;
nè motti oscuri o parolette amene;
nè dire io feci, io fui, io andai, io stetti.

Al primo si domanda, chi l'ha fatto:
e in sul nome di quel si fa 'l giudizio.
Non avvien questo al pingere o sculpire:

se l'opra è buona, si conosce a un tratto;
nè importa aver del mastro prima indizio.
Sculpite or voi: e noi lasciate dire.

The Bales of Sonnets

The bales of sonnets are now quite well collected,
With very few of them considered fine.
All poets know the truth to come in this one
Because they've summoned the muses—with few elected.

It doesn't count that its conceits are well selected,
Or show love in its ecstasies and pain,
Or strange devices, or a well phrased tone,
Or saying, "I was, I went, I lived, I have perfected."

The first thing always asked is this: who wrote it?
And judgment's based upon his name's allure.
In painting and sculpture there's no such doubletalk.

If work is good, you know it in a minute.
It's not important, some master's signature.
So why don't you go sculpt—and let us talk.

Faustina Maratti Zappi (1679?–1745)

Sonetto

Donna, che tanto al mio bel Sol piacesti,
che ancor de' pregi tuoi parla sovente,
lodando ora il bel crine, ora il ridente
tuo labbro, ed ora i saggi detti onesti;

dimmi, quando le voci a lui volgesti,
tacque egli mai, qual uom che nulla sente?
o le turbate luci alteramente,
come a me volge, a te volger vedesti?

De' tuoi bei lumi alle due chiare faci
io so ch'egli arse un tempo, e so che allora . . .
Ma tu declini al suol gli occhi vivaci?

Veggo il rossor, che le tue guance infiora,
parla, rispondi, ah non risponder, taci,
taci, se mi vuoi dir ch'ei t'ama ancora!

Sonnet

Woman, because my sun-man liked you so,
Often speaking of you with admiration,
Or praising your fine hair, the glad vibration
Of your pure lips, the wisdom that you show,

Tell me: when you turned to talk with my beau,
Was he never silent, a man who feels no passion?
Or did you catch his eyes in haughty elation
As he turned on you, the way he does me too?

From your two lovely eyes, clear as your will,
I know he's burned a while, and know you two . . .
But you just drop your eyes? Those eyes that kill?

I see the red that floods your cheeks, I do.
Respond—say something—don't—be still, be still
If you still want to tell me he loves you!

Gabriele D'Annunzio (1863–1938)

L'ala sul mare

Ardi, un'ala sul mare è solitaria.
Ondeggia come pallido rottame.
E le sue penne, senza più legame,
sparse tremano ad ogni soffio d'aria.

Ardi, veggo la cera! È l'ala icaria,
quella che il fabro della vacca infame
foggiò quando fu servo nel reame
del re gnòssio per l'opera nefaria.

Chi la raccoglierà? Chi con più forte
lega saprà rigiugnere le penne
sparse per ritentare il folle volo?

Oh del figlio Dedalo alta sorte!
Lungi dal medio limite si tenne
il prode, e ruinò nei gorghi solo.

The Wing on the Sea

Ardi, a desolate wing floats on the sea.
It waves about, a ghostly ragged sheet.
And its feathers, without their binding more complete,
Tremble with each puff of air, set free.

Ardi, it's Icarus' wing! It's wax I see!—
His wing, that the cow-maker made beat
When he crudely performed his service to the state
Of the King of Knossus, with criminal infamy.

Who'll gather it? Who, with a braver skin,
Will know how to rebind the scattered feathers
And continue on the foolish flight again?

Oh, the lofty fate of Daedalus' son!
The brave holds court above the reach of others
And plunges headlong into gulfs alone.

Umberto Saba (1883–1957)

Di ronda alla spiaggia

Annotta. Nella piazza i trombettieri
uscirono a suonar la ritirata.
La consegna io l'ho, credo, scordata;
che tendono a ben altro i miei pensieri.

E il mare solitario i miei pensieri
culla con le sue lunghe onde grigiastre,
dove il tramonto scivolò con piastre
d'oro, rifulse in liquidi sentieri.

Questo a lungo ammirai, ben che al soldato
più chiudere che aprire gli occhi alletta,
che ha i piedi infermi ed il cuore malato.

E seggo, e sulla sabbia umida e netta
un nome da infiniti anni obliato
scrive la punta della baionetta.

Beach Patrol

Night falls. The army buglers in the square
Are moving out to sound the day's retreat.
The orders I have, I think, I may forget.
My thoughts reach out to something far more rare.

And the lonely sea makes a cradle for my despair
With its long and grizzly and wavy beat
Where its mournful fall, with coins of plate
Like gold, reflects long liquid paths from shore.

How long I loved this. It more easily dares
The soldier to open his eyes than keep them shut,
Moving nervously with heartsick fears.

And I sit down, and on sand clean and wet
A name forgotten now for countless years
Inscribes itself with my sharp bayonet.

GERMAN SONNETS

Andreas Gryphius (1616–1664)

Tränen des Vaterlandes

Wir sind doch nunmehr ganz, ja mehr dann ganz verheeret!
Der frechen Völker Schar, die rasende Posaun,
Das vom Blut fette Schwert, die donnernde Karthaun
Hat aller Schweiß und Fleiß und Vorrat aufgezehret.

Die Türme stehn in Glut, die Kirch ist umgekehret,
Das Rathaus liegt im Graus, die Starken sind zerhaun,
Die Jungfraun sind geschänd't, und wo wir hin nur schaun,
Ist Feuer, Pest und Tod, der Herz und Geist durchfähret.

Hier durch die Schanz und Stadt rinnt allzeit frisches Blut;
Dreimal sind's schon sechs Jahr, als unsrer Ströme Flut,
Von Leichen fast verstopft, sich langsam fortgedrungen;

Doch schweig' ich noch von dem, was ärger als der Tod,
Was grimmer denn die Pest und Glut und Hungersnot:
Daß auch der Seelen Schatz so vielen abgezwungen.

Lament for His Homeland

Right now we're not just wholly, but more than wholly, in hell.
The crazy mass of people, the raging battle horn,
The sword greased with blood, the thundering royal gun
Have eaten up all our sweat and toil and war matériel.

The towers loom through embers, the church sounds its own death
                                        [knell,
The government waits in dread, the strong are chopped right down,
The women have been assaulted, and everywhere we turn
Are flames, plague and death, piercing heart, and spirit as well.

The trenches and city streets run daily with fresh blood.
It's three times six years here since our river's lazy tide—
Now almost stopped up with corpses—followed its casual rolls.

But I still haven't noted the thing that's fouler by far than death,
Far worse than the plague and embers and famine across the earth:
That so many have also seen plundered the treasure of their souls.

Gottfried August Bürger (1747–1794)

An das Herz

Lange schon in manchem Sturm und Drange
Wandeln meine Füße durch die Welt.
Bald, den Lebensmüden beigestellt,
Ruh' ich aus von meinem Pilgergange.

Leise sinkend faltet sich die Wange;
Jede meiner Blüten welkt und fällt.
Herz, ich muß dich fragen: Was erhält
Dich in Kraft und Fülle noch so lange?

Trotz der Zeit Despoten-Allgewalt
Fährst du fort, wie in des Lenzes Tagen,
Liebend wie die Nachtigall zu schlagen.

Aber ach! Aurora hört es kalt,
Was ihr Tithons Lippen Holdes sagen.—
Herz, ich wollte, du auch würdest alt!

An Address to the Heart

For so long now, through so much storm and stress,
My feet have led me roaming far and wide.
Soon, with all world-weariness laid aside,
I'll put an end to my pilgrim-like express.

My cheek contracts, soft-sinking in some distress,
My flowers—all—have withered or have died.
So—heart—I've got to ask you: what blind pride
Sustains your strength and joy through this excess?

Despite omnipotent time's quite ruthless hold,
You go right on, as you did in early days,
Like a nightingale, enjoying your beating ways.

But oh, Aurora hears you and she's cold
To what her Tithonus' voice so gently says:
"I hoped, my heart, that you too might grow old!"

Johann Wolfgang von Goethe (1749–1832)

Das Sonett

Sich in erneutem Kunstgebrauch zu üben,
Ist heil'ge Pflicht, die wir dir auferlegen.
Du kannst dich auch, wie wir, bestimmt bewegen,
Nach Tritt und Schritt, wie es dir vorgeschrieben.

Denn eben die Beschränkung läßt sich lieben,
Wenn sich die Geister gar gewaltig regen;
Und wie sie sich denn auch geberden mögen,
Das Werk zuletzt ist doch vollendet blieben.

So möcht' ich selbst in künstlichen Sonetten,
In sprachgewandter Maße kühnem Stolze,
Das Beste, was Gefühl mir gäbe, reimen;

Nur weiß ich hier mich nicht bequem zu betten:
Ich schneide sonst so gern aus ganzem Holze,
Und müßte nun doch auch mitunter leimen.

You, Sonnet

To push oneself into fresh artistic use
Is blessed business—just what we ask of you.
Like us, and step by step, you can release
Most surely—yourself, as you were meant to do.

For it's just the constraint that is enjoyed
If spirits rule themselves with sweeping power,
And since just then they're also well deployed
Their work at last may find its fullest flower.

That's what I want myself in lovely sonnets,
To rhyme the best that feelings send my way
In fluent measures full of my proud soul—

Only I know myself too well to accept warm blankets:
I'd rather carve from whole wood any day,
And now would sometimes have to glue the whole.

Johann Wolfgang von Goethe

Natur und Kunst

Natur und Kunst, sie scheinen sich zu fliehen
Und haben sich, eh man es denkt, gefunden;
Die Widerwille ist auch mir verschwunden,
Und beide scheinen gleich mich anzuziehen.

Es gilt nur ein redliches Bemühen!
Und wenn wir erst, in abgemessnen Stunden,
Mit Geist und Fleiß uns an die Kunst gebunden,
Mag frei Natur im Herzen wieder glühen.

So ist's mit aller Bildung auch beschaffen:
Vergebens werden ungebundne Geister
Nach der Vollendung reiner Höhe streben.

Wer Großes will, muß sich zusammenraffen;
In der Beschränkung zeigt sich erst der Meister,
Und das Gesetz nur kann uns Freiheit geben.

Nature and Art

Nature and art—they seem to split and flee
And find each other before one thinks about it.
My stubbornness too has been completely routed
So right now both seem to appeal to me.

What's missing is only an honest preparation!
The fact is that if we first devote hard hours—
Of spirit, of work—to art, accepting its powers,
The heart once more feels nature's illumination.

That's how it goes with every transformation:
All struggles to reach the perfection of airy summits
Prove useless to spirits feeling only liberty.

Whoever wants what's best seeks combination:
A master first reveals himself in limits,
And law alone can truly set us free.

August von Platen (1796–1835)

Venedig

I

Mein Auge ließ das hohe Meer zurücke,
Als aus der Flut Palladios Tempel stiegen,
An deren Staffeln sich die Wellen schmiegen,
Die uns getragen ohne Falsch und Tücke.

Wir landen an, wir danken es dem Glücke,
Und die Lagune scheint zurückzufliegen,
Der Dogen alte Säulengänge liegen
Vor uns gigantisch mit der Seufzerbrücke.

Venedigs Löwen, sonst Venedigs Wonne,
Mit ehrnen Flügeln sehen wir ihn ragen
Auf seiner kolossalischen Kolone.

Ich steig ans Land, nich ohne Furcht und Zagen,
Da glänzt der Markusplatz im Licht der Sonne:
Soll ich ihn wirklich zu betreten wagen?

Venice

I

My eyes let all the high seas fall away
As Palladio's temples rose up from the tide—
At whose steps the waves pretend to hide,
Waves that brought us here without foul play.

We reach the pier, relieved, in real surprise,
And all the lagoon appears to fly straight backwards.
Old columns of the Doges reach out towards
Us, like giants, with the Bridge of Sighs.

We see the Lion of Venice, once its proud glory,
Spreading the noble passions of its wings
On its colossal columned promontory.

I step ashore, a bit afraid of things—
There's Saint Mark's Square, aglow in sunlit fury—
And do I dare encounter its summonings?

August von Platen

Venedig

II

Dies Labyrinth von Brücken und von Gassen,
Die tausendfach sich ineinander schlingen,
Wie wird hindurchzugehn mir je gelingen?
Wie werd ich je dies große Rätsel fassen?

Ersteigend erst des Markusturms Terrassen,
Vermag ich vorwärts mit dem Blick zu dringen,
Und aus den Wundern, welche mich umringen,
Entsteht ein Bild, es teilen sich die Massen.

Ich grüße dort den Ozean, den blauen,
Und hier die Alpen, die im weiten Bogen
Auf die Laguneninseln niederschauen.

Und sieh! da kam ein mut'ges Volk gezogen,
Paläste sich und Tempel sich zu bauen
Auf Eichenpfähle mitten in die Wogen.

Venice

II

This labyrinth of bridges, this alley-muddle
That slithers about itself with a thousand coils—
How shall I ever navigate its folds?
Or solve, if I'm allowed, this giant riddle?

Climbing Saint Mark's tower to its terraced places,
I was able to look ahead, to push beyond me,
And out of the marvels stretching all around me
A picture forms, composed of all their masses.

I greet the ocean over there, the blue one,
And here the Alps that on the distant plain
Regard the islands of the vast lagoon,

And see them coming—a people, brave, in droves,
To build themselves the palace-temple town
On oak-piles in the middle of the waves.

Heinrich Heine (1797–1856)

Friedrike (1823)

Verlaß Berlin, mit seinem dicken Sande,
Und dünnen Tee, und überwitz'gen Leuten,
Die Gott und Welt, und was sie selbst bedeuten,
Begriffen längst mit Hegelschem Verstande.

Komm mit nach Indien, nach dem Sonnenlande,
Wo Ambrablüten ihren Duft verbreiten,
Die Pilgerscharen nach dem Ganges schreiten,
Andächtig und im weißen Festgewande.

Dort, wo die Palmen wehn, die Wellen blinken,
Am heil'gen Ufer Lotosblumen ragen
Empor zu Indras Burg, der ewig blauen;

Dort will ich gläubig vor dir niedersinken,
Und deine Füße drücken, und dir sagen:
Madame! Sie sind die schönste aller Frauen!

To Frederika (1823)

Give up Berlin, with its thick (shifting) sand
And thin tea and over-witty people of fashion
Who long ago worked out with Hegelian passion
What heaven and earth, and they themselves, portend.

Come on to India, to the sunny south
Where the amber-blossoms broadcast their perfume,
Where pilgrim crowds along the Ganges hum
Devoutly, wearing their white festive cloth.

There, where the palm trees blow, the waves shine true,
On the holy bank the lotus blossoms reach
High toward Indra's citadel, blue forever—

There shall I faithfully kneel down to you
And embrace your feet and make a simple speech:
Madam, you are the prettiest woman ever!

Ricarda Huch (1864–1947)

Der Verbannte

Der Abend grüßt das Tal; ihr feuchtes Schlafgemach
Betritt die Sonne froh auf der vertrauten Bahn.
Zum Ufer wieder lenkt der Schiffer seinen Kahn;
Schon winkt ihm durch das Grün ein wohlbekanntes Dach.

Gern wallt die Herde heim, dem müden Hirten nach.
Die Sorg und Müh und Last, den ruhelosen Wahn
Vergißt die Seele nun, der Heimat Bilder nahn,
Und freud'ge Sehnsucht wird in jedem Busen wach.

Wem aber ewig sich das Vaterland verschlossen,
Der sucht sich andre Wege. Wenn im dunklen Spiegel
Des Sees erloschen schon der Glanz der Silberfirne,

Zieht er noch seinen öden Pfad. Ihm sind Genossen
Nachtvögel nur, die freudlos flattern; denn das Siegel
Der Einsamkeit trägt er auf der umwölkten Stirne.

The Exiled

Twilight greets the valley. The easy sun rolls in,
Into that humid bedroom, on its familiar track.
Once more the skipper poles his bank-bound boat straight back.
Already a well known roof salutes him through the green.

Behind the weary herdsman, the herd sweeps home again.
All worries, conflicts, pains, illusions like a rack—
The soul dismisses. Images of home collect
And a joyful yearning stirs the heart of everyone.

But for the person banned forever from old haunts—
He must seek other ways. When in the darkened glass
Of the lake the gleams dissolve of powdery snow

He keeps along his alien path. His only friends
Are night birds coldly flapping—for he bears the trace
Of solitude, a seal, upon his twilight brow.

Rainer Maria Rilke (1875–1926)

Dame vor dem Spiegel

Wie in einem Schlaftrunk Spezerein,
löst sie leise in dem flüssigklaren
Spiegel ihr ermüdetes Gebaren;
und sie tut ihr Lächeln ganz hinein.

Und sie wartet, daß die Flüssigkeit
davon steigt; dann gießt sie ihre Haare
in den Spiegel und, die wunderbare
Schulter hebend aus dem Abendkleid,

trinkt sie still aus ihrem Bild. Sie trinkt,
was ein Liebender im Taumel tränke,
prüfend, voller Mißtraun; und sie winkt

erst der Zofe, wenn sie auf dem Grunde
ihres Spiegels Lichter findet, Schränke
und das Trübe einer späten Stunde.

Lady before her Mirror

As into a spicy nightcap, she comes to place
Softly now, into her true-flowing true
Mirror her exhausted afterglow,
And then she sends her smile quite into the glass.

And she waits until the clearest flowing truths
Push out of it, then pours her loosened hair
Into the mirror, and tossing her wonderful bare
Shoulder straight out of her evening clothes,

Drinks calmly of her image. And oh, she drinks
As a lover in some ecstasy might drink,
Testing, full of mistrust, and only winks

To her maid when she finds in the weakening power
Of her mirror electric lights, and chests in a rank,
And the encroaching shadows of the hour.

Rainer Maria Rilke

Gesang der Frauen an den Dichter

Sieh, wie sich alles auftut: so sind wir;
denn wir sind nichts als solche Seligkeit.
Was Blut und Dunkel war in einem Tier,
das wuchs in uns zur Seele an und schreit

als Seele weiter. Und es schreit nach dir.
Du freilich nimmst es nur in dein Gesicht,
als sei es Landschaft: sanft und ohne Gier.
Und darum meinen wir, du bist es nicht,

nach dem es schreit. Und doch, bist du nicht der,
an den wir uns ganz ohne Rest verlören?
Und werden wir in irgendeinem mehr?

Mit uns geht das Unendliche vorbei.
Du aber sei, du Mund, daß wir es hören,
du aber, du Uns-Sagender: du sei.

The Women Sing to the Poet

See how all things rise: that's how we are,
For we are nothing other than salvation.
The blood and darkness of some beast earlier
Becomes sheer soul in us and cries elation

As soul expanding—and it cries your need.
Of course you simply take it into your face
That seems its landscape: gentle and without greed.
And so we often think you're not the place

For which it cries. And yet—aren't you the one
In whom we utterly would lose ourselves?
And aren't we made more by your every tone?

We're simply scanted by Infinity.
But you—pure Voice—would be its hearing-valves.
But you—pure Us-Sayer—would simply be.

Rainer Maria Rilke

Der Tod des Dichters

Er lag. Sein aufgestelltes Antlitz war
bleich und verweigernd in den steilen Kissen,
seitdem die Welt und dieses von ihr Wissen,
von seinen Sinnen abgerissen,
zurückfiel an das teilnahmslose Jahr.

Die, so ihn leben sahen, wußten nicht,
wie sehr er eines war mit allem diesen,
denn dieses: diese Tiefen, diese Wiesen
und diese Wasser waren sein Gesicht.

O sein Gesicht war diese ganze Weite,
die jetzt noch zu ihm will und um ihn wirbt;
und seine Maske, die nun bang verstirbt,
ist zart und offen wie die Innenseite
von einer Frucht, die an der Luft verdirbt.

Death of the Poet

He languished. His presented countenance
Was faint and stubborn among the sloping pillows,
As the world and knowledge of its fellows,
Torn from his mind's hollows,
Fell away into that year of indifference.

Those who saw him living did not guess
How much he was at one with all of this,
And for this reason: its deeps, its meadowed grass
And its very waters were his very face.

His face was all the planet far and wide
That even now seeks him out and begs reply,
And his mask that even now must softly die
Is tender and open like the soft inside
Of a fruit left out and spoiling against the sky.

Rainer Maria Rilke

Der Tod der Geliebten

Er wußte nur vom Tod, was alle wissen:
Daß er uns nimmt und in das Stumme stößt.
Als aber sie, nicht von ihm fortgerissen,
nein, leis aus seinen Augen ausgelöst,

hinüberglitt zu unbekannten Schatten,
und als er fühlte, daß sie drüben nun
wie einen Mond ihr Mädchenlächeln hatten
und ihre Weise wohlzutun:

da wurden ihm die Toten so bekannt,
als wäre er durch sie mit einem jeden
ganz nah verwandt; er ließ die andern reden

und glaubte nicht und nannte jenes Land
das gutgelegene, das immersüße—.
Und tastete es ab für ihre Füße.

Death of his Beloved

Of death he only knew what all men know:
That he takes us and stuffs us into the maze.
But when she was not torn from him, ah, no,
But softly loosening from his softening eyes

Glided over among unfamiliar spirits
And when he saw that these might now include
Like a moon her smiling girlish merits
And even her way of doing good:

Then all the dead felt suddenly close at hand,
As if he were through her with every ghost
Closely related; he let the world protest

And refused to listen and called her Other Land
The well disposed, the everlastingly sweet—
And groped about it, smoothing it for her feet.

Rainer Maria Rilke

Archäischer Torso Apollos

Wir kannten nicht sein unerhörtes Haupt,
darin die Augenäpfel reiften. Aber
sein Torso glüht noch wie ein Kandelaber,
in dem sein Schauen, nur zurückgeschraubt,

sich hält und glänzt. Sonst könnte nicht der Bug
der Brust dich blenden, und im leisen Drehen
der Lenden könnte nicht ein Lächeln gehen
zu jener Mitte, die die Zeugung trug.

Sonst stünde dieser Stein entstellt und kurz
unter den Schultern durchsichtigem Sturz
und flimmerte nicht so wie Raubtierfelle

und bräche nicht aus allen seinen Rändern
aus wie ein Stern: denn da ist keine Stelle,
die dich nicht sieht. Du mußt dein Leben ändern.

Ruined Torso of Apollo

We never knew his quite outrageous face
In which his eyes like apples ripened. But
His torso, like a candelabra, glows
With his gaze anyhow, just more discreet

And waiting, shining. Otherwise that barrel
Of his chest could hardly blind you, and the smile
In the soft ripple of his hips could hardly travel
Straight to his center bearing his sexual guile.

And even this marble would seem a crippled crush
Under his shoulders' transparent downwards rush
And hardly glisten like some wild beast's pelt

And like a star becoming a shining knife
Burst all its bounds: for there's no part unfelt
And not seeing you: You've got to change your life.

Georg Trakl (1887–1914)

Verfall

Am Abend, wenn die Glocken Frieden läuten,
Folg ich der Vögel wundervollen Flügen,
Die lang geschart, gleich frommen Pilgerzügen,
Entschwinden in den herbstlich klaren Weiten.

Hinwandelnd durch den dämmervollen Garten
Träum ich nach ihren helleren Geschicken
Und fühl der Stunden Weisen kaum mehr rücken.
So folg ich über Wolken ihren Fahrten.

Da macht ein Hauch mich von Verfall erzittern.
Die Amsel klagt in den entlaubten Zweigen.
Es schwankt der rote Wein an rostigen Gittern,

Indes wie blaßer Kinder Todesreigen
Um dunkle Brunnenränder, die verwittern,
Im Wind sich fröstelnd blaue Astern neigen.

Decay

In the evening, as the bells proclaim pure graces,
I follow the birds' fine airy passages
That form long lines, like serious pilgrimages,
Vanishing into autumnal glassy spaces.

Wandering through the twilight-filling garden,
I long for their far brighter-destined living
And feel the hour's rustle barely moving.
I soar the clouds to follow where they are bidden.

A breath of air shivers in me like decay.
The blackbird mourns among the desolate branches.
The red vine flickers against the rusty fences

While like pale children bowing in death dances
Around dark mouths of wells crumbling away
Blue chilling asters accept the wind's cold glances.

Marie Louise Kaschnitz (1901–1974)

Geduld

Geduld. Gelassenheit. O wem gelänge
Es still in sich in dieser Zeit zu ruhn,
Und wer vermöchte die Zusammenhänge
Mit allem Grauen von sich abzutun?

Zwar blüht das Land. Die reichen Zweige wehen,
Doch Blut und Tränen tränken rings die Erde
Und in der Tage stillem Kommen, Gehen
Verfällt das Herz der tiefsten Ungebärde.

Und ist des Leidens satt und will ein Ende
Und schreit für Tausende nach einer Frist,
Nach einem Zeichen, daß das Kreuz sich wende.

Und weiß doch nicht, mit welchem Maß der Bogen
Des Unheils über dieser Welt gezogen
Und welches Schicksal ihm bereitet ist.

Patience

Patience. Calm. For whom—oh—are there occasions
In this age to be quietly calm inside?
And who can brush aside the situations
Of all imaginable forms of dread?

The land blooms anyway. The lush boughs sway,
Though blood and tears were streaming round the earth
And in the quiet come and go of day
The human heart falls into the wildest wrath.

And has had enough of sorrow and wants an end
And cries, for thousands, for a deadline of some sort,
Some sign the burden may be overturned.

And doesn't know how tautly may be pulled
The bow of disaster drawn across the world
And what new fate may now await the heart.

FRENCH SONNETS

Maurice Scève (ca. 1501–ca. 1563)

En grace du Dialogue d'Amour, et de Folie, Euvre de D. Louïze Labé, Lionnoize

Amour est donq pure inclinacion
Du Ciel en nous, mais non necessitante:
Ou bien vertu, qui nos coeurs impuissante
A resister contre son accion?

C'est donq de l'ame une alteracion
De vain desir legerement naissante
A tout objet de l'espoir perissante,
Comme muable à toute passion?

Ja ne soit crû, que la douce folie
D'un libre Amant d'ardeur libre amollie
Perde son miel en si amer Absynte,

Puis que lon voit un esprit si gentil
Se recouvrer de ce Chaos sutil,
Ou de Raison la Loy se laberynte.

In Honor of a Dialogue on Love and Madness,
A Work of Lady Louïze Labé of Lyon

So is love, then, the purest infiltration
Of Heaven into us, but no firm trap?
Or some fine strength that leaves our hearts to grope
In making real resistance to its action?

Is love, then, a soul's mere new direction
Through vain desire springing fast and cheap
For any object of mere dying hope,
As changeable as every passing passion?

Beyond belief is that the sweet mad passion
Of some free lover who offers free devotion
Should lose its sweets to acid like absinthe

Because the noblest lover is seen to be
Emerging from that cunning anarchy
Where sense flees reason in a labyrinth.

Pierre de Ronsard (1524–1585)

XLIII (*Sonnets pour Hélène,* Livre II)

Quand vous serez bien vieille, au soir à la chandelle,
　Assise auprez du feu, devidant et filant,
　Direz chantant mes vers, en vous esmerveillant,
　Ronsard me celebroit du temps que j'estois belle.

Lors vous n'aurez servante oyant telle nouvelle,
　Desja sous le labeur à demy sommeillant,
　Qui au bruit de Ronsard ne s'aille resveillant,
　Bénissant vostre nom de louange immortelle.

Je seray sous la terre et fantôme sans os
　Par les ombres myrteux je prendray mon repos;
　Vous serez au fouyer une vieille accroupie,

Regrettant mon amour et vostre fier desdain.
　Vivez, si m'en croyez, n'attendez à demain,
　Cueillez dès aujourdhuy les roses de la vie.

Sonnet XLIII (Book II of *Sonnets for Helen*)

By candlelight one evening, when you are very old,
Sitting beside your fire, winding skeins and spinning your wheel,
You'll say, singing my lines, and marveling as well,
"Ronsard praised all my charms when I was pretty to behold."

You won't have any servant girls who, as they hear that news
                                        [unfold,
Already half-asleep at work, nearby you in your shawl,
Won't wake up at the sound of "Ronsard" that you'll call,
Blessing your name made deathless by the praise my lines retold.

I'll be beneath the earth by then, a ghost sans flesh and bone,
Among the myrtle shadows, taking my rest alone.
You'll just be an old woman, crouched at the fire's rosy play,

My love and your hard scorn just bringing you fresh sorrow.
So live, if you believe me, and forget about tomorrow
And gather up the roses of your life right now, today.

Joachim du Bellay (1522–1560)

Sonnet

Si notre vie est non moins qu'une journée
En l'éternel, si l'an qui fait le tour
Chasse nos jours sans espoir de retour,
Si périssable est toute chose née,

Que songes-tu, mon âme emprisonnée?
Pourquoi te plaît l'obscur de notre jour,
Si pour voler en un plus clair séjour
Tu as au dos l'aile bien empanée?

Là est le bien que tout esprit désire,
Là le repos où tout le monde aspire,
Là est l'amour, là le plaisir encore.

Là, ô mon âme, au plus haut ciel guidée,
Tu y pourras reconnaître l'Idée
De la beauté qu'en ce monde j'adore.

Sonnet

If life is no more than a day's sojourn
Into the eternal, if the year's relentless turn
Hunts down our days sans hope of their return,
If perishable is everything that's born,

For what, my pent-up soul, do you still yearn?
Why do you enjoy our passage here forlorn
If you've still on your back a wing unshorn
And feathered for flight into a brighter morn?

There is the good that every spirit desires,
There the peace to which everyone aspires,
There the love, and there the pleasure too.

There, my soul, led to a heaven more real,
You can at last encounter the Ideal
Of Beauty that in this world I worship so.

Gérard de Nerval (1808–1855)

Antéros

Tu demandes pourquoi j'ai tant de rage au coeur
Et sur un col flexible une tête indomptée;
C'est que je suis issu de la race d'Antée,
Je retourne les dards contre le dieu vainqueur.

Oui, je suis de ceux-là qu'inspire le Vengeur,
Il m'a marqué le front de sa lèvre irritée,
Sous la pâleur d'Abel, hélas! ensanglantée,
J'ai parfois de Caïn l'implacable rougeur!

Jéhovah! le dernier, vaincu par ton génie,
Qui du fond des enfers, criait: 'O tyrannie!'
C'est mon aïeul Bélus ou mon père Dagon . . .

Ils m'ont plongé trois fois dans les eaux du Cocyte,
Et protégeant tout seul ma mère Amalécyte,
Je ressème à ses pieds les dents du vieux dragon.

Anteros

You ask why I've got so much rage at heart
And a head indomitable over a neck that's bowed.
It's because I'm from Antaeus' race, apart.
I fling back arrows at the triumphant One God.

In fact, I'm one of those who fires His vengeance.
He's branded my forehead with His searing lips.
Beneath my paleness of Abel—Christ, the blood-drops!—
I've sometimes got the red print of Cain's passions.

Jehovah: the last one to be crushed by Your mastery,
Who shrieks from the depths of hell, "Oh, tyranny!"
That's my ancestor Baal or my father Dagon . . .

Three times they've plunged me in Cocytus' water—
And protecting alone the Amalekite, my mother,
I resow at her feet the teeth of the old dragon.

125

Paul Verlaine (1844–1896)

Sonnet boiteux

Ah! vraiment c'est triste, ah! vraiment ça finit trop mal.
Il n'est pas permis d'être à ce point infortuné.
Ah! vraiment c'est trop la mort du naïf animal
Qui voit tout son sang couler sous son regard fané.

Londres fume et crie. O quelle ville de la Bible!
Le gaz flambe et nage et les enseignes sont vermeilles.
Et les maisons dans leur ratatinement terrible
Epouvantent comme un sénat de petites vieilles.

Tout l'affreux passé saute, piaule, miaule et glapit
Dans le brouillard rose et jaune et sale des Sohos
Avec des *indeeds* et des *all rights* et des *haôs*.

Non vraiment c'est trop un martyre sans espérance,
Non vraiment cela finit trop mal, vraiment c'est triste:
O le feu du ciel sur cette ville de la Bible!

Limping Sonnet

It's really sad—oh, it's really ending quite badly.
It isn't possible to live through this dismal phase.
It's really too much a dumb beast's dumber death, sadly,
That sees all its blood running out beneath its blurred gaze.

London smokes and screams. What a city of the Bible!
The gas lamps flare and swim and the shop signs are crimson.
And the houses, in their shriveling, so terrible,
Terrify like a senate of little old women.

All horror past leaps out, whimpers, meows and gibbers
In the pink and yellow and filthy fog that's Soho's
With all these "indeeds" and these "all rights" and these "aye-os."

It's really too much a martyrdom without hope.
It's really ending too badly. It really is sad:
Oh—the fire of heaven on this city of the Bible!

Arthur Rimbaud (1854–1891)

Le dormeur du val

C'est un trou de verdure où chante une rivière
Accrochant follement aux herbes des haillons
D'argent; où le soleil, de la montagne fière,
Luit: c'est un petit val qui mousse de rayons.

Un soldat jeune, bouche ouverte, tête nue,
Et la nuque baignant dans le frais cresson bleu,
Dort; il est étendu dans l'herbe, sous la nue,
Pâle dans son lit vert où la lumière pleut.

Les pieds dans les glaïeuls, il dort. Souriant comme
Sourirait un enfant malade, il fait un somme:
Nature, berce-le chaudement: il a froid.

Les parfums ne font pas frissonner sa narine;
Il dort dans le soleil, la main sur sa poitrine
Tranquille. Il a deux trous rouges au côté droit.

The Sleepyhead of the Valley

It's a green hole here, a glen, where a river sings
Through the grass, madly tossing its tatters
Of silver—where the sun, from the arrogant mountains,
Shines: a little valley frothing with glitters.

A soldier, young, mouth open, his head bare
And his nape swimming in the fresh blue watercress
Sleeps; he's spread out under the sky, in the grass,
White in his green bed, where light pours there.

With his feet in the gladioli, he sleeps. Smiling
As a sick baby might, he looks beguiling—
Nature, rock him with your heat. He's cold.

The fragrances won't make his nostrils thirst.
He sleeps here in the sun, hand on his chest,
At peace. He's got two red holes in his side.

Albert Samain (1858–1900)

Cléopâtre

Accoudée en silence aux créneaux de la tour,
La Reine aux cheveux bleus serrés de bandelettes,
Sous l'incantation trouble des cassolettes,
Sent monter dans son coeur ta mer, immense Amour.

Immobile, sous ses paupières violettes
Elle rêve, pâmée aux fuites des coussins,
Et les lourds colliers d'or soulevés par ses seins
Racontent sa langueur et ses fièvres muettes.

Un adieu rose flotte au front des monuments,
Le soir, velouté d'ombre, est plein d'enchantements;
Et cependant qu'au loin pleurent les crocodiles,

La Reine aux doigts crispés, sanglotante d'aveux,
Frissonne de sentir, lascives et subtiles,
Des mains qui dans le vent épuisent ses cheveux.

Cleopatra

Leaning in silence at the rampart of her tower,
The queen, her blue hair piled in chains of coils,
Under the censers chanting for lost souls,
Feels you, love, rise in her heart, your sealike power.

Inert beneath her eyelids' purple covers,
She dreams, swooning among her pillows, drifting,
And on her breasts her weighty gold chains, lifting,
Describe her indolence and quiet fevers.

A pink farewell drifts over the monuments,
The evening, shadow-brushed, is full of enchantments.
And while off in the distance the crocodiles cry,

The queen, weeping over her crimes, wringing her hands,
Shivers to feel, salacious, teasingly,
New hands exhaust her hair into the winds.

Paul Valéry (1871–1945)

L'Abeille

Quelle, et si fine, et si mortelle,
Que soit ta pointe, blonde abeille,
Je n'ai, sur ma tendre corbeille,
Jeté qu'un songe de dentelle.

Pique du sein la gourde belle,
Sur qui l'Amour meurt ou sommeille,
Qu'un peu de moi-même vermeille
Vienne à la chair ronde et rebelle!

J'ai grand besoin d'un prompt tourment:
Un mal vif et bien terminé
Vaut mieux qu'un supplice dormant!

Soit donc mon sens illuminé
Par cette infime alerte d'or
Sans qui l'Amour meurt ou s'endort!

The Bee

How sharp, how deathly terse
Is knowing your sting, blond bee:
I've never, on my soft body's basketry,
Thrown more than a dream of lace.

Sting the gourd of my breast, so flush,
On which love dies or drowses
So a trace blood-red as it rouses
Shows on my full and rebellious flesh.

I crave some quick ambush of pain:
A sickness that's sharp and complete
Is worth more than some torture that's plain—

So my senses know the bright beat
Through the gold of that live leap
When love neither dies nor can sleep.

Vincent Muselli (1880–1957)

Les banlieues

Vieux murs pleins de venin, routes empoisonnées,
Pour ton coeur inquiet c'est ici qu'il fait bon:
Vois s'étendre, au delà des vapeurs du charbon,
Un horizon haineux peuplé de cheminées!

Débris honteux, métaux tordus dans la fureur,
Vont de leur noir cadavre insultant la campagne;
Tout n'est que rouille et lèpre, et seule t'accompagne
D'un sol martyrisé la désertique horreur.

Ah! laisse les jardins, les fleurs et leurs mensonges,
O mon Vérane, et va porter tes libres songes
Jusqu'à ces carrefours de chaos et de mort!

Le soleil égorgé saigne dans les prairies,
Là-bas; et monte en nous, ivresse et réconfort,
La douce odeur du sang qui vient des boucheries.

The Outskirts of the City

Old walls full of decay, polluted streets—
Here's the perfect place for your anxious heart;
See how the hateful horizon falls apart,
Peopled with chimneys, where the black smoke floats.

Vile scraps, steel towers bent in angry air,
Insulting the landscape with their heaved black corpse,
It's all just rust and peeling—and the desert collapse
Of a martyred land appalls you everywhere.

Get out of those gardens and flowers and their lies,
Vérane, my dear, and bring your fantasies
Straight over to these crossroads of chaos and death.

On meadows there the knifed sun bleeds huge drops—
But drunk and easy, we'll soak up with each breath
The sweet stench of real blood from butcher shops.

SPANISH SONNETS

Juan Boscán (1493?–1542)

Soneto LXXVIII

Antes terné que cante blandamente,
pues amo blandamente, y soy amado;
sé que en amor no es término forzado,
sólo escribir aquel que dolor siente.

Desaváhase quien está doliente,
y canta en la prisión el desdichado,
con hierros y cadenas fatigado;
mas su cantar del nuestro es diferente.

Yo cantaré conforme al avecilla,
que canta así a la sombra de algún ramo,
que el caminante olvida su camino,

quedando trasportado por oílla.
Así yo de ver quien me ama y a quien amo,
en mi cantar terné gozo contino.

Sonnet LXXVIII

Now delicacy suits my singing best
Because I love—am loved—with delicacy.
I know now that in love it isn't necessary
Merely to see hard painful things expressed.

Any man in pain must sing about his pain
And a man in prison sings whole canticles
About his fetters and weary manacles—
But this my song is something else again.

I'd like to sing just like that little bird
That sings well in the shadow of some branch,
So well that any hiker loses his way

Distracted by the music that he's heard.
So I, through seeing who loves me that much,
And whom I love, make songs of endless joy.

Luis de Góngora (1561–1627)

57 (1582)

Al tramontar del Sol la Nimpha mia,
  De flores despojando el verde llano,
  Quantas troncaba la hermosa mano,
  Tantas el blanco pie crecer hacia.

Ondéàbale el viento que corria
  El oro fino con error galano,
  Qual verde oja de alamo loçano
  Se mueue al roxo despuntar de'l dia.

Mas luego que ciñò sus sienes bellas
  De los varios despojos de su falda,
  (Termino puesto al oro, i a la nieue)

Iurarè, que luciò mas su guirnalda,
  Con ser de flores, la otra ser de estrellas,
  Que la que illustra el cielo en luces nueue.

57 (1582)

My woman makes the sun hide over the hill,
Stripping the flowers from the greenest lea—
As many as her lovely hand pulls free
Her whitest foot makes grow till they overspill.

The wind that rises manages to thrill
Her hair's pure gold with careless gallantry,
Much as the green leaf of the poplar tree
Shivers aside as dawn's red starts to spill.

But when she garlanded her temples' glory
From folds of her skirt with all that pilfered wealth
(So parting her gold from her forehead's snow-delights)

I'd swear the sudden brightness of her wreath
Though made of flowers, while the heavenly wreath is starry,
Shone brighter than Ariadne's with its nine lights.

Lope de Vega (1562–1635)

Soneto II

Cuando imagino de mis breves días
los muchos que el tirano amor me debe
y en mi cabello anticipar la nieve
más que los años las tristezas mías,

veo que son sus falsas alegrías
veneno que en cristal la razón bebe
por quien el apetito se le atreve
vestido de mis dulces fantasías.

¿Qué hierbas del olvido ha dado el gusto
a la razón que sin hacer su oficio
quiere contra razón satisfacelle?

Mas consolarse quiere mi disgusto,
que es el deseo del remedio indicio
y el remedio de amor querer vencelle.

Sonnet II

When I consider the shortness of my days—
How love (the tyrant) owes me such a slew—
And that my hair expects a lot of snow,
More than the sorrows of past years gone their ways,

I see the falsities of all their joys
Are poison reason drinks as a dazzling brew
Because that's what sheer thirst can make it do
Dressed in my sweet crystal fantasies.

What spiced amnesia gave my mind this passion
For craving pleasure contrary to good sense
Without performing its duty rationally?

But my annoyance brightens with the notion
That it's the desire for medicine in this case,
And the medicine for love is victory.

Lope de Vega

IV

Era la alegre víspera del día
que la que sin igual nació en la tierra
de la cárcel mortal y humana guerra
para la patria celestial salía;

y era la edad en que más viva ardía
la nueva sangre que mi pecho encierra
cuando el consejo y la razón destierra
la vanidad que el apetito guía,

cuando amor me enseñó la vez primera
de Lucinda en su sol los ojos bellos
y me abrasó como si rayo fuera.

Dulce prisión y dulce arder por ellos;
sin duda que su fuego fué mi esfera,
que con verme morir descanso en ellos.

IV

It was the happy eve of that holiday
When she, born with no equal on this earth,
Departed this mortal prison and living death
For her celestial realm for which we pray.

It was the time of the most burning play
My chest could hold of my new blood, sheer youth,
When care and reason gave the widest berth
To vanity that shows appetite the way—

When love, to me, for the first time then, revealed
Lucinda's sun with her two beautiful eyes—
As if it were a ray, I felt it scald.

For them, this prison's hot sweet intensities—
Without a doubt her fire was my world:
I'll live in them, and die as worms may please.

Miguel de Unamuno (1864–1936)

Junto a la Laguna del Cristo, en la Aldehuela de Yeltes, Una noche de luna llena

Noche blanca en que el agua cristalina
duerme queda en su lecho de laguna
sobre la cual redonda llena luna
que ejército de estrellas encamina

vela, y se espeja una redonda encina
en el espejo sin rizada alguna;
noche blanca en que el agua hace de cuna
de la más alta y más honda doctrina.

Es un rasgón del cielo que abrazado
tiene en sus brazos la Naturaleza;
es un rasgón del cielo que ha posado

y en el silencio de la noche reza
la oración del amante resignado
sólo al amor, que es su única riqueza.

Near the Lake of Christ in Aldehuela de Yeltes: A Night of Full Moon

White night in which the water, crystal clear,
Sleeps peacefully within its bed of lake,
Above which the moon, round, brimming and awake
And ordering the army of stars up there

Stands guard, and a round oak glances, self-aware,
Into the mirror that no ripples break—
White night, in which the water seems to make
A cradle for the highest deepest lore.

The water is a shred of sky that nature,
Embracing, holds within its powerful arms,
A shred of heaven like a settled feature

And in the silent night the water forms
The prayer the lover speaks resigned to venture
On love alone, as all the wealth he claims.

Antonio Machado (1875–1939)

Sonetos

I

Tuvo mi corazón, encrucijada
de cien caminos, todos pasajeros,
un gentío sin cita ni posada,
como en andén ruidoso de viajeros.

Hizo a los cuatro vientos su jornada,
disperso el corazón por cien senderos
de llana tierra o piedra aborrascada,
y a la suerte, en el mar, de cien veleros.

Hoy, enjambre que torna a su colmena
cuando el bando de cuervos enronquece
en busca de su peña denegrida,

vuelve mi corazón a su faena,
con néctares del campo que florece
y el luto de la tarde desabrida.

Sonnets

I

My heart, a crossroads of a hundred roads helter-skelter,
Once accepted everyone passing through,
A mass of people with neither goals nor shelter—
As in a station where travelers gossip and go.

It made its journey to all four winds ascatter
And sent itself, my heart, down a hundred paths too,
On flat ground, and stony, where the wild storms batter,
And the chancy sea, where a hundred fast ships flew.

Today, a swarm returning to its hive
Whenever the flock of ravens shouts itself hoarse
Searching for its cliff-like blackened stone,

My heart turns to its task as in a wave,
With nectars from the field's huge flower bursts
And grief of the late bitter afternoon.

Antonio Machado

IV

Esta luz de Sevilla . . . Es el palacio
donde nací, con su rumor de fuente,
Mi padre, en su despacho.—La alta frente,
la breve mosca, y el bigote lacio—.

Mi padre, aún joven. Lee, escribe, hojea
sus libros y medita. Se levanta;
va hacia la puerta del jardín. Pasea.
A veces habla solo, a veces canta.

Sus grandes ojos de mirar inquieto
ahora vagar parecen, sin objeto
donde puedan posar, en el vacío.

Ya escapan de su ayer a su mañana;
ya miran en el tiempo, ¡padre mío!,
piadosamente mi cabeza cana.

IV

This light of Seville . . . There's the manor estate
Where I was born, with its fountain's liquid sigh.
My father in his office.—His forehead high,
His terse goatee, his mustache stiff and straight.

My father, still young. He reads, he writes, leafs through
His books and thinks. He rises among his things.
He nears the garden gate. Goes through it now.
Sometimes he talks alone, sometimes he sings.

His large eyes, their expression vaguely abject,
Now seem to wander, with no finite object
On which to fix, into the vacant Other—

Already fleeing today for his tomorrow,
Already staring time down—oh, my father!—
My head turns gray in most devout sweet sorrow.

Juana de Ibarbourou (1895–1979)

Rebelde

Caronte: yo seré un escándalo en tu barca.
Mientras las otras sombras recen, giman, o lloren,
y bajo tus miradas de siniestro patriarca
las tímidas y tristes, en bajo acento, oren,

yo iré como una alondra cantando por el río
y llevaré a tu barca mi perfume salvaje,
e irradiaré en las ondas del arroyo sombrío
como una azul linterna que alumbrara en el viaje.

Por más que tú no quieras, por más guiños siniestros
que me hagan tus dos ojos, en el terror maestros,
Caronte, yo en tu barca seré como un escándalo.

Y extenuada de sombra, de valor y de frío,
cuando quieras dejarme a la orilla del río,
me bajarán tus brazos cual conquista de vándalo.

The Rebel

Charon, I'll be a scandal in your barque.
While other ghosts are weeping, whining, swaying,
And under your glare as evil patriarch
The sad and frightened whimper in their praying,

I'll wander singing, a lark along the river
And drench your boat with my animal perfume
And see to it my light makes dark waves shiver—
Like a blue lantern shining on our foam.

No matter how you beg, how much the horrors
Hound me from your eyes with master-terrors—
Charon, I'll leave your ferry scandalized.

And exhausted with the gloom, with courage and cold,
When you try to let me off on the other side,
Your arms will drop me ravished, vandalized.

Federico García Lorca (1899–1936)

Adán

Árbol de sangre moja la mañana
por donde gime la recién parida.
Su voz deja cristales en la herida
y un gráfico de huesco en la ventana.

Mientras la luz que viene fija y gana
blancas metas de fábula que olvida
el tumulto de venas en la huída
hacia el turbio frescor de la manzana.

Adán sueña en la fiebre de la arcilla
un niño que se acerca galopando
por el doble latir de su mejilla.

Pero otro Adán oscuro está soñando
neutra luna de piedra sin semilla
donde el niño de luz se irá quemando.

Adam

The blood tree soaks for hours well past dawn
Where, lately delivered, the woman continues to howl.
Her voice leaves splinters of glass in the wound's hole
And an outline of bone in the windowpane.

Meanwhile the light that comes can set and gain
White limits for the tale—it forgets it tells
Of the passionate surge of veins in the flight that swells
Toward the apple's chilling threat of pain.

Adam dreams, in the clay that seems to bake,
A boy who rushes at him there, careens,
Because of the double throbbing of his cheek.

But another darker Adam also dreams—
A neutral stone moon where no seed can take,
Where the child of light goes up in ferocious flames.

Notes on the Poets and Poems

GIACOMO DA LENTINO

Sonnets IX and X. A number of Giacomo's earliest sonnets employ tag words rather than rhymes, as is the case here. The goal is to achieve a pleasure equivalent to that of rhymes, through the skillful juxtaposition of the different meanings of the same word.

Sonnet XXVIII. The basilisk, swan, peacock, and phoenix are here described according to medieval superstitions. The peacock was thought to be embarrassed by the frightening ugliness of its feet.

[Reply to Jacopo Mostacci and Pier della Vigna.] Giacomo's description of a love that depends on vision for its existence, and his association of it with the divine love that "runs the whole world's natural order," is typical of contemporary courtly love lyrics.

DANTE ALIGHIERI

Sonnet XI. The "ghosts demented" ("spiriti paurosi") of line 9 are not simply fears but qualities of perception or mind. In *La vita nuova* (xiv, 14), for instance, Dante speaks of love as "killing all my spirits" ("Amor uccide tutti li miei spiriti").

FRANCESCO PETRARCA

Rime sparse: 164 and 165. The decline of Petrarch's formidable reputation over the past century is due to justifiable accusations of decorativeness and bombast. The decline has also obscured a more balanced estimate of him as a poet of great subtlety, beauty, and originality. His influence on such poets as Ariosto, Michelangelo, Lope de Vega, Góngora, Ronsard, Sidney, and Donne was considerable, and throughout Europe he was perceived as having liberated poetry from constricting medieval attitudes, in his *Rime sparse* and *Trionfi*. From a twentieth-century point of view, this perception often seems ill supported by a style that combines wit, elegance, frequent preciosity, and abstraction with undying passion for his legendary mistress, Laura, whose very existence is problematic. The brilliant obscurity of the image of the nocturnal bird, in the last line of the sonnet numbered 165, may be regarded as typical, both for its fascination and difficulty. The poet here compares a night bird's inability to refrain from gazing at the sun with the dazzling sun-like effect produced on him by the face of his beloved (Laura).

MICHELANGELO BUONARROTI

Sonnet CXLVII. "Erroneously, as Frey has demonstrated, this famous sonnet was believed dedicated to Vasari [whose *Lives of the Painters, Sculptors, and Architects* was first published in 1550, and who was Michelangelo's friend]: in fact, the poet [here] at the close of his life, collects himself, in a humble and profound devotional, divorcing himself from all worldly sentiments and preparing to meet his death as a true Christian." G. R. Ceriello, ed., Michelangelo Buonarroti, *Rime* (Milan, 1954), p. 272.

FAUSTINA MARATTI ZAPPI

The daughter of Carlo Maratti, a famous painter, and born in Rome, she married the poet Giambattista Felice Zappi in 1705, and herself wrote numerous sonnets.

GABRIELE D'ANNUNZIO

D'Annunzio's *Primo Vere* (1879), *Canto Novo* (1881), *L'Intermezzo di Rime* (1884), and his major work in poetry, the three-volume *Laudi* (1903–4), established him as an important Italian poet. His chief work for the theater, *La Figlia di Jorio,* also dates from 1904. D'Annunzio was extremely active and popular politically, as an ardent Italian nationalist who opposed Fascism.

The Wing above the Sea (L'ala sul mare). The "cow-maker" ("fabro della vacca") in lines 6–8 is Daedalus, Icarus' father and the maker of Icarus' famous wings. Having murdered Talos in Athens, Daedalus fled to Crete, where he was welcomed by King Minos. He enjoyed the king's favors and hospitality until it was discovered that he had built the cow that enabled Pasiphaë, Minos' queen, to mate with Poseidon's white bull. Imprisoned for his crime, in the Labyrinth, together with his son, Daedalus was freed by Pasiphaë. To escape Crete altogether, he fashioned wings for himself and Icarus, stitching the quill feathers together but binding the small ones with wax. Ardi is a figure in *Alcione* (1904).

ANDREAS GRYPHIUS

Although Gryphius is among the earliest sonneteers to appear in Germany, Christoph Wirsung is the first to introduce the Italian form into the language. His (1550) translation of a sonnet by the Reformation priest Bernardino Ochino (1487–1564) follows the familiar Italian rhyme scheme abba-abba-cde-cde. It received scant attention. Georg Rudolf Weckherlin (1584–1653), who was born in Stuttgart, took an English wife, and died in London, is perhaps the first poet of significance to write a body of sonnets in German. Weckherlin's sonnets reveal an acquaintanceship with his Italian predecessors, and an even greater familiarity with French and English sonnet literature. His sonnets were first published in Amsterdam in 1648, the last year of the Thirty Years' War (Weckherlin had moved to England in 1616, when the war began). By this time, Martin Opitz (1597–1639), influenced by Ronsard's alexandrine lines, which were also popular with poets in Leiden, where Opitz had gone to study, had already published a group of sonnets in German. To Opitz, therefore, belongs the distinction of being the first influential German composer of sonnets. Opitz, though not as good a poet as Weckherlin, was more influential in the area of theory as well. He advocated the alexandrine line as clearly superior to the *vers commun* of the ten-syllable, or iambic pentameter, line, and in doing so set the style of German sonneteering for generations. Andreas Gryphius, undoubtedly the finest poet of this early Baroque group of German sonneteers, retained the alexandrine lines favored by Opitz, but introduced two new and interesting themes, the spiritual and social. In sonnets such as **Lament for**

his Homeland (Tränen des Vaterlandes), he combines a worldly vision of the barbarities of the Thirty Years' War with profound spiritual convictions. From a thematic point of view, his poetry is comparable to Lope de Vega's *Rimas sacras* and to sonnets of Milton. It breaks rather sharply with the courtly sonnets of Weckherlin and the drier, duller verse of Opitz. Gryphius' *Hundert Son- und Feiertagssonette* was published when he was twenty-three.

GOTTFRIED AUGUST BURGER

The son of a country parson, Bürger became a professor at Göttingen. He is usually regarded as the most gifted of the young Sturm und Drang poets, who espoused ideals similar to those of Jefferson and Rousseau and sought the recreation of a popular German poetry. Most famous for his *Lenore* (1773), which was translated by Sir Walter Scott, Bürger was one of the first poets to revive the sonnet in modern German literature (in fact he may be the first).

An Address to the Heart (An das Herz). Tithonus (l. 13), son of Laomedon, King of Troy, was so handsome that Aurora, goddess of the dawn, fell in love with him. She bore him off, promising him immortality, a boon which he cheerfully accepted. But he had forgotten to ask for eternal youth, and soon became old and weak. He begged Aurora to remove him from this world. Since he had been rendered immortal (an apparently unchangeable condition), she responded by turning him into a grasshopper.

JOHANN WOLFGANG VON GOETHE

You, Sonnet (Das Sonett) and **Nature and Art (Natur und Kunst).** Goethe wrote relatively few sonnets. The first dates from the end of the eighteenth century, the second from a few years later, when with German classicism at its height, romanticism makes its appearance. The poems present the classical-romantic conflict, and also the poet's shift in attitude toward it.

AUGUST VON PLATEN

Born in Ansbach, in Bavaria (he died in Syracuse, in Sicily), Platen is commonly considered the finest of modern German writers of sonnets, with the possible exception of Rilke. His sonnet cycle *Sonette aus Venedig,* consisting of seventeen sonnets, of which the first two are translated here, is perhaps his most perfect work, influencing deeply the poetry of Herwegh and Liliencron. Platen himself was deeply influenced by Shakespeare's sonnets. The cycle *Sonette aus Venedig* was completed on October 20, 1824, following his first visit to Italy.

RAINER MARIA RILKE

Rilke's commitment to the sonnet extends throughout his career, and includes translations (1908) of Elizabeth Barrett Browning's *Sonnets from the Portuguese* and twenty-four sonnets by the French Renaissance poet Louïze Labé (see Maurice Scève, below). Deeply influenced by French symbolist poets such as Verlaine (see Verlaine, below) and Mallarmé, Rilke introduces new rhythms and rhyme schemes into the Italian and French forms of the sonnet, to which he basically adheres, especially in his often translated *Sonnets to Orpheus.* A similarly potent mixture of innovations may be discerned in the sonnets here translated, in which off rhymes crisscross with traditional iambics, and hexameters with dactyls, trochees, and iambs, and the sort of exact rhymes that would have attracted August von Platen.

MAURICE SCÈVE

While it is debatable who first introduced the sonnet into French (in the 1540s), Scève was among the first, as well as among the most influential and best. Petrarch, a powerful guiding force for the earliest French writers of sonnets, was translated by Vasquin Philieul in 1548. Plato's *Ion* appeared in 1546, embodying for French poets such as Sebillet, Ronsard, and du Bellay (see Ronsard and du Bellay, below) a theory of poetry that was to become prominent. This theory, which for a time influenced early members of the group of poets known as La Pléiade, among them Ronsard and du Bellay, stressed the imprisonment of the soul in the body as a theme suitable for poetry, and the contrast between an ideal and a real world, coming down heavily on the side of the ideal. Scève, along with Louïze Labé (often called "la Sapho lyonnaise"; her sonnets have been ably translated into modern English by Graham Dunstan Martin, and for this reason are not included here), was important among the poets of Lyon immediately preceding La Pléiade. Scève's *Délie*, written in *dizains* rather than sonnets, owes much to Petrarch and less to Plato.

In Honor of a Dialogue on Love and Madness, A Work by Lady Louïze Labé of Lyon (En grace du Dialogue d'Amour, et de Folie, Euvre de D. Louïze Labé, Lionnoize). Louïze Labé published her poetry in book form in 1555. This volume also contained her *Le Débat de folie et d'amour*. The debate, or dialogue, as Scève refers to it in his title, is in prose and is accompanied by twenty-four poems by other poets, among them Scève, who contributed the sonnet translated here. The poem presents a number of familiar scholastic, or Platonistic, usages. *Inclinacion* (l. 1) refers to the influences, or "infiltrations," of astral as well as heavenly powers. *Vertu* (l. 3) is an important term throughout Scève's poetry, and refers both to the virtue possessed by the noble spirit and the power granted such a person by God. Both the "infiltration" and the virtue, or strength, were therefore physical and personal as well as spiritual. They controlled to some extent the behavior of human beings, as is implied by the Boethian *non necessitante* of line 2. Scève speculates on the greatness of the extent, or the free will that any lover may be presumed to have. While it was a settled issue among medieval and Renaissance poets, and nearly everyone else, that humanity possessed some free will, Boethius had long ago demonstrated that absolute free will was impossible and incomprehensible. As Lucifer could not choose to become God, so a man could not decide to change himself into an angel or an ostrich. On the other hand, the law of divine reason (the *Raison* of l. 14), making for an orderly universe, must somehow reign supreme. Scève rather typically raises the question whether the lover has enough freedom to make a real resistance to love's *accion* (l. 4). His conclusion is that if the lover is of noble birth (the *esprit si gentil* of l. 12) and therefore has character, he may save himself from the labyrinth of disorder that other lovers will surely experience. The reference to the absinthe-like bitterness (or acid) that lies in wait for lovers who have no character and who freely change the objects of their passions is a paraphrase of Prov. 5:3–4: "car les lèvres de l'étrangère distillent le miel . . . mais à la fin elle est amère comme l'absinthe" ("for the lips of the strange woman drip with honey . . . but her end is bitter as absinthe").

PIERRE DE RONSARD

With Ronsard and La Pléiade, there occurs in French poetry a complete rejection of all that may be considered medieval, including verse forms and subject matter. In their place, as a deliberate substitution, is the inspirational guidance of the recovered authors of the ancient Greek and Roman world, especially Plato (see also Maurice Scève, above). Ronsard's *Odes* (1550–52) demonstrated a thorough acquaintanceship with such classical models as Horace and Pindar. These poems also break with the traditional medieval verse forms of the ballade and rondeau, introducing a flexibility that increases with the poet's *Amours de Cassandre* (1552), a group of love poems in the Petrarchan vein, though the lines are decasyllabic. *Les Amours de Marie* (1555–56) marks the first continuous use of the alexandrine, or twelve-syllable line. It had an enormous influence on poets and dramatists in France ever after. The harmonic beauty and naturalness of this line in French have been compared with the naturalness of the iambic pentameter in English. Efforts to develop the alexandrine sonnet in German proved most successful with Andreas Gryphius (see Gryphius, above).

Sonnet XLIII, Book II of Sonnets for Helen (Sonnets pour Hélène, Livre II, XLIII). Book I of Ronsard's sonnets to Hélène de Surgères contains fifty-four sonnets, Book II seventy-seven, together with "Stances" (meant to be sung or recited by three performers) and an "Elégie" (included in Book II for the first time in 1584). Both books were published as new additions to the fifth edition of Ronsard's collected works (1578), though the poet apparently began to write them perhaps as early as 1570. The concrete personal details, amounting to a definition of the character of Hélène as well as the poet himself in this famous sonnet, as in many others, are novel and unique—and in striking contrast to the more generalized images of Laura to be found in Petrarch.

JOACHIM DU BELLAY

Du Bellay, a friend of Ronsard (see Ronsard and Scève, above), published his important *La Deffence et Illustration de la Langue Françoise* in the same year (1549) as he published *L'Olive,* the first sonnet sequence in French. The *Deffence,* which relies heavily on Latin and Italian authorities, solidly attacks medieval forms and traditions. It amounts to a manifesto for the new French poetry produced by La Pléiade, and is Platonistic and Petrarchan in outlook and aesthetics, respectively.

Sonnet. The poem, from *L'Olive,* reflects du Bellay's characteristic themes of longing, of the soul as a prisoner in the body, and of the possibility of a flight after death into a Platonistic realm of ideal beauty.

GERARD DE NERVAL

Anteros. The theme of this allusive poem is the task of Nerval as poet: to devote himself to the rebirth of a pagan Golden Age by helping to topple Jehovah, the "One God" of line 4. The poet presents himself, first, as Anteros, the pagan or pre-Christian son of Gaea, goddess of the earth, and Poseidon, god of the sea. Anteros is thus a figure representative of this world rather than the next. His attitude is one of pure defiance. In the second quatrain, the speaker identifies himself with another defiant figure, Cain, the primordial murderer, who is to be understood as a provoker of God's vengeance and as an avenger (both meanings are implicit in the original; the French translation of the Bible casts Cain in the role of avenger). Anteros, as well, is an avenger of unrequited love. The first tercet extends the poet's genealogy to include Baal and Dagon, "false" gods banished by Jehovah to the underworld, with its five rivers, among them Cocytus, the river of wailing. In the final tercet, the poet has become the lonely guardian of his exiled Amalekite mother (the Amalekites, according to Exod. 17: 8–17, were disinherited by God). The last line shows the poet as a figure like Cadmus, who after slaying a dragon, planted its teeth, from which grew the founders of the city of Thebes, or a new and literate civilization (Cadmus introduced the use of letters into Greece). The entire poem anticipates, in tone and revolutionary spirit, Zarathustra's announcement in Nietzsche's *Also Sprach Zarathustra* (1883) that "God is dead."

PAUL VERLAINE

Limping Sonnet (Sonnet boiteux). Based on a thirteen-syllable line that limps and jerks about in an impressionistic enactment of its ideas and images, the poem reveals a straining beyond form and toward modernism. The reasons for the speaker's misery are never made clear, deliberately. The association of the speaker's misery with horrifying perspectives of London and a wounded animal (l. 4) watching its own blood stream from its body parallels the collapse of the poem's rhyme scheme in the last six lines. Yet the despair combines with fiery rage. The reference to London as the "city of the Bible" (perhaps a hint of Verlaine's having read poems of Blake), the call for London's incendiary destruction—in an act of divine arson—turn the whole into a vision of apocalypse.

ARTHUR RIMBAUD

The Sleepyhead of the Valley (Le dormeur du val). Written when Rimbaud was sixteen, the sonnet is surely meant to capture something of the horror of the Franco-Prussian War (1870–71). Notable here, from the viewpoint of the sonnet's growing expansion of idiom and the new directions it was to take, are the flat journalistic tone and the journalistic punchiness of the last, and surprising, eight words.

ALBERT SAMAIN

Usually regarded as a minor Symbolist poet, Samain is remarkable for the striking originality of his images that, as François Coppée has said, exhale "l'odeur faible et mélancholique, le parfum d'adieu des crysanthèmes" ("the weak and melancholy fragrance, the perfume of farewell of chrysanthemums").

PAUL VALÉRY

The Bee (L'Abeille). Valéry's truncation of the sonnet's usual decasyllabic line matches perfectly the stinging, erotic brevity of the experience presented, and anticipates a time in which content would dictate, or eliminate (depending on one's point of view), form for many poets.

VINCENT MUSELLI

Muselli published several collections of sonnets: *Les Sonnets à Philis, Les Sonnets Moraux,* and *Sonnets* (brought together in *Points et Contrepoints,* Paris, 1957). Between 1909 and 1914, when the First World War forced its closing, he was, with prominent poets such as Apollinaire, a regular contributor to *Les Marges,* a combative journal founded by the Friends of Latin and devoted to perpetuating literary freedom of expression in the tradition of Rabelais, Voltaire, and Stendhal.

JUAN BOSCÁN

Boscán's visits to Italy resulted in his adoption of Italian forms in his poetry, including that of the sonnet, which he introduced into Spanish literature. His translation of Castiglione's *The Courtier* became the source of a polite aristocratic tone among generations of Spanish writers.

LUIS DE GÓNGORA

As the chief exponent of the movement in seventeenth-century Spanish poetry known as *culteranismo,* Góngora and his followers favored a style, meant for the *cultos* or educated, that mingled a deliberately "poetic" vocabulary with obscure metaphors and often difficult syntax. The intention was to imitate, and "make modern," revered Latin poets, frequently through allusions to classical mythology. Góngora's gifts of imagery and poetic power shine through this approach, which may seem daunting to twentieth-century readers. In fact his influence in the twentieth century has been considerable, especially on what has been termed the Generation of 1927 (the three-hundredth anniversary of Góngora's death), including Dámaso Alonso, Jorge Guillén, and Vicente Aleixandre.

57 (1582). The image of the foot that magically makes flowers grow in a meadow (ll. 3–4) echoes Petrarch's quite similar image, in his Sonnet 165 (ll. 3–4; see pp. 72–73). The reference in line 14 is to Ariadne, who lent Theseus the thread by which he could find his way out of the Labyrinth after killing the Minotaur, and who was deserted by Theseus at Naxos. She married Dionysus, who set her bridal crown among the stars. The crown consists of one major and nine minor stars.

LOPE DE VEGA

The greatest genius of the Spanish theater of the "Golden Age," Lope de Vega may have written as many as 2,000 plays, in every genre, of which 352 survive. All of Lope de Vega's extant sonnets—843 of them—are to be found within the texts of his plays.

IV. The reference in line 1 is to the Feast of the Annunciation (March 25).

MIGUEL DE UNAMUNO

Receiving a doctorate in classical philology at the age of twenty from the University of Madrid, Unamuno's career combined poetry, fiction, criticism, scholarship, and politically, intense opposition to the Fascist regime of Franco.

Near the Lake of Christ in Aldehuela de Yeltes: A Night of Full Moon (Junto a la Laguna del Cristo, en la Aldehuela de Yeltes, Una noche de luna llena). Lines 1, 5, and 6 are distant echoes of two lines in the *First Eclogue* of the poet Garcilasco de la Vega (1503?–36): "Corrientes aguas, puras, cristalinas; / árboles que os estáis mirando en ellas" ("Rushing waters, pure, crystal clear; / trees reflecting on yourselves in them").

ANTONIO MACHADO

Machado is often compared with Rilke, for both the meditational and experimental, or modernist, qualities of his poetry. In fact Spanish modernism owes much to Baudelaire and Verlaine (see Verlaine, above) as well as to South American writers such as José Martí, Asunción Silva, and especially Rubén Darío (1867–1916) of Nicaragua. Refusing to describe himself as either a "clasico o romantico," in his *Retrato* (*Self-Portrait*), Machado identifies himself perhaps more closely with the "fuente vasco" ("hardy Basque"), or Miguel Unamuno, as Machado refers to the older poet in *The Life of Don Quixote and Sancho*.

JUANA DE IBARBOUROU

Las lenguas de diamante (1919), *El cantaro fresco* (1920), *Raiz salvaje* (1922), *La rosa de los vientos* (1930), and *Perdida* (1950) have established Ibarbourou as one of the most popular and influential poets of Uruguay.

FEDERICO GARCÍA LORCA

Adam (Adán). Lorca wrote few sonnets. Here, as in the rest of his widely known poetry, he combines intense personal symbolism with surrealism. In the sestet, Adam's dreams of the doom-filled destiny of his son Abel contain elements familiar to readers of Lorca's less formal verse—blood, wounds, flames—that add up to a fearful commentary on the temptation scene in Genesis (referred to in l. 8).

III

Scholarly Background:
The Origin of the Sonnet

The Origin of the Sonnet

A good deal of the mystery surrounding the origin of the sonnet was cleared up by Ernest Hatch Wilkins in 1915. In his fine investigative piece "The Invention of the Sonnet,"[1] Wilkins establishes, as well as they can be established from the skimpy evidence available, two important facts: one, that the earliest sonnets were written by Giacomo da Lentino, *il Notaro* (as he is often called by his contemporaries, and as Dante refers to him in *Purgatorio,* XXIV .56), who lived ca. 1188–1240, was a notary in the service of Frederick II, and appears to have created the form; and two, that in writing the earliest sonnets Giacomo did not borrow from the troubadours' eight-line *canzone* for the octave of his poems, or indeed from Provençal literature at all, but from the eight-line *strambotto,* familiar as a song form among thirteenth-century Sicilian peasants—so that we must today, if we wish to be accurate about the matter, regard the sonnet as Italian, and even Sicilian, in origin.

In his 1915 essay, Wilkins speculates that the sestet of Giacomo's sonnets may have derived from the Arab *zajal,* a rhyming stanza popular with the Arabs living in Sicily in Giacomo's time. Wilkins abandons this idea as "negligible," however, in a subsequent essay,[2] in which he argues that the sestet came to Giacomo in a burst of sheer inspiration.[3] No research done since 1915 has revealed an alternative source of the sestet, nor has anyone chal-

1. "The Invention of the Sonnet," Modern Philology, 13 (1915), 463–94. Previous studies of the sonnet may be found in Karl Witte's preface to *Hundert Sonette von Eugen Baron von Vaerst und zwei Freunden* (Breslau, 1825) and H. Welti, *Geschichte des Sonettes in der deutschen Dichtung* (Leipzig, 1884). For a detailed account of the first—mostly useless—historical research see Wilkins, p. 466, n. 1.

2. Ernest Hatch Wilkins, *The Invention of the Sonnet and Other Studies in Italian Literature* (Rome, 1959), p. 35.

3. Wilkins, *Invention,* p. 38.

lenged Wilkins' opinion. Indeed, his opinion—that Giacomo spon-
taneously added six rhyming lines to a previously existing eight-
line form to produce the new form of the sonnet—is crucial in
many ways to what I wish to explore. For much of the mystery
surrounding the first sonnets remains. It seems clear enough that if
we can manage to understand, much better than we do now, the
circumstances of Giacomo's inspiration, and perhaps even the motives that lay behind it, we may increase our understanding not
only of those important developments in early thirteenth-century
Italian poetry which were shortly to lead to the *stilnovisti* poems
of Dante and Petrarch, but also of the history of Western poetry
itself. For the invention of the sonnet was a momentous event.
Since Giacomo, few major poets—one is urged to say, few minor
ones too—in Italian, German, French, Spanish, and English have
failed to write sonnets.[4] What is more, the gathering esteem in
which this "scanty plot of ground," as Wordsworth put it, has
been held by poets, critics, and readers over the past seven centuries suggests that the sonnet's mysterious aesthetic perfection
probably amounts in importance to the revelation of a psychologi-
cal, as well as an aesthetic, law, or equation, or archetype: the
sonnet, like the profoundest of small mirrors, still plumbs the
depths of our best poets' richest gifts,[5] and it is probably what
the literary historian thinks of first when he thinks of secure and

4. Walter Mönch's comments on the universality of the form, in his book
Das Sonett: Gestalt und Geschichte (Heidelberg, 1955), p. 11, are worth
quoting: "Nearly all lyric poets of the Old and New World have written
sonnets. Among the great ones, there is but a small band—to it belong
Schiller, Bellman, Leopardi, Hölderlin, Walt Whitman—that has paid the
sonnet no homage. Moreover, not all peoples have received the sonnet into
the body of their lyric poetry with the same enthusiasm. In addition to lin-
guistic reasons, there have been various historical, social, political, and in-
tercultural-psychological conditions influential on this apparently independent development of European sonnet culture. Beyond this, the picture
changes over the course of centuries. Countries into whose body of lyric
poetry the sonnet at first found access difficult, such as (to some extent)
Spain, sooner or later blossomed with a flowering of sonnets." [All translations mine unless otherwise noted; hereafter cited in the text.]

5. It is surely pertinent to recall that Yeats' "Leda and the Swan," Robert
Frost's "Design," as well as countless more recent and often successful
poems by innumerable living poets in many countries, are in fact sonnets.

enduring forms in poetry. In this study I would like to suggest that the invention of the sonnet may possess an even greater importance: it may mark the beginnings of what we must mean by "modern" poetry, a term whose redefinition I shall discuss in the final section.

The importance of the sonnet has not, of course, always been recognized. Wordsworth himself opens his second sonnet (published in 1827) with a rebuke to scornful critics: "Scorn not the sonnet; Critic, you have frowned, / Mindless of its just honours." In fact much of the disdain heaped on the form, as well as a good deal of the foolishness that has been written about it, stems from a set of misunderstandings, both of the form itself and of its intentions. The whole matter may appear differently once we begin to view familiar facts in new ways. These facts fall into three general categories—the name "sonnet" itself, the contents and themes of Giacomo's earliest sonnets, and the milieu of the court of Frederick II—each of which requires consideration here.

It has been universally assumed by critics and lexicographers that the word "sonnet" means "little song," or more properly "little sound," and that it derives from *suono,* meaning "sound," with the *-etto* suffix acting as a diminutive. Thus John Fuller, whose book *The Sonnet* is one of the best summaries of sonnet criticism to date, speaks of "the sonnet's original musical setting";[6] while one of the earliest practitioners of the form in England, George Gascoigne, writes with an authority which, however unsupported in fact, echoes through all criticism of the form from the sixteenth to the twentieth centuries: "Then haue you Sonnets: some thinke that all Poemes (being short) may be called Sonets, as in deede it is a diminutiue worde deriued of *Sonare,* but yet I can beste allowe to call those Sonnets whiche are of fouretene lynes, every line conteyning tenne syllables."[7] The conviction that the word "sonnet" somehow means "song," and that the sonnet must somehow, even in its infancy, have been regarded as "musical," or designed for ac-

6. *The Sonnet* (London, 1972), p. 5; hereafter cited in the text.
7. "Certayne Notes of Instruction Concerning the Making of Verse or Rhyme in English" (1575), in *Elizabethan Critical Essays,* ed. G. Gregory Smith (Oxford, 1904), p. 55.

tual music composed specifically for the sonnet at hand—that in other words any sonnet ought somehow to be considered an explicit invitation to performable music—may be found, if only by implication, in these remarks by Walter Mönch on the musical history of the sonnets of Petrarch:

> We do not know whether Petrarch sang his sonnets, and how the musical settings were obtained—if such a thing even existed in the *trecento*. The oldest-preserved musical settings are not sonnets, but madrigals, ballads, and *caccie*. Moreover, prior to Petrarch, verses by Cavalcanti, Dante, Donati, and Boccaccio had already been set to music. The musical setting of the Petrarchan sonnet "Pace non truovo e non ho da far guerra" dates only from about the year 1470. (pp. 82–83)

Mönch, like the editor of *Sonetti della scuola siciliana,* Edoardo Sanguineti, whose introduction to his collection of the sonnets of the Sicilian school is notable for its argument that the sonnet in its earliest appearances (with Giacomo, Pier della Vigna, and Jacopo Mostacci, for instance) is really a sort of epistle, wishes to believe that all sonnets, not simply those of Petrarch, demand a musical setting and are in fact somehow "little songs." Sanguineti sees the sonnet as a type of recitative, a declamatory poem that falls between singing and ordinary speech: "The recitative of the sonnet, as we may term it, in contrast to the aria of the *canzone,* is a lifting, in its best moments, to a type of recited singing, or in more modern terminology, of spoken song [*Sprechgesang*]."[8] Sanguineti's view is surely commonly—one is tempted to say, rather too easily—accepted. The logic runs this way: the octave of the sonnet derives from a musical form, the *strambotto;* the performable and musically accompanied lyrics of the troubadours were well known to Giacomo and must have influenced him indirectly to produce his variation, which we call the sonnet and which must be regarded as a species of poetry that is somehow "musical" and "performable"; therefore the sonnet itself may, indeed must, be seen as a type of *Sprechgesang,* as a spoken song, a poem intended both for music and for an audience accustomed to hearing its poetry sung. This reasoning is reinforced, in the English tradition

8. *Sonetti della scuola siciliana* (Turin, 1965), p. 5.

at least, by such statements as Sidney's "Other sorts of Poetry almost haue we none, but that Lyricall kind of Songs and Sonnets"[9] and Leigh Hunt's:

> [The sonnet] derived its name, like the composition called a *Sonata, from being sounded* or played; that is to say, accompanied by a musical instrument. To *sound*, in Italian, still means to play music; and the sonnet, of old, was never without such accompaniment . . . The sonnet, agreeably to its appellation, was never heard without the sounding of the lute or the guitar. This connection, as we shall see, lasted a long time; and when it ceased, it left upon the little poem a demand for treatment more than commonly musical, and implying, so to speak, the companion which it had lost.[10]

But it is precisely in reading such statements, including one by Mario Praz,[11] that a puzzle arises. The puzzle is really twofold. In the first place, there is no evidence whatever to support the notion that Giacomo and his contemporaries of the Sicilian school thought of their sonnets as recitatives or *Sprechgesänge,* or poems intended in any way for music. In the second place, a certain amount of evidence is available to us which suggests (a) that the word "sonnet" may not be derived directly from *suonare* or *suono,* and (b) that it may have meant something quite different to Giacomo and those other early Italian sonneteers who were his immediate successors. Sidney, Hunt, and that considerable army of poets, critics, and scholars who see the sonnet as essentially musical (in the sense that it begs for actual music as an accompani-

9. Sir Philip Sidney, "An Apologie for Poetrie," ca. 1583 (printed 1595); see Smith, p. 201.

10. *The Book of the Sonnet,* ed. Leigh Hunt and S. Adams Lee (Boston, 1867), I, pp. 8–9.

11. See *The Flaming Heart* (Garden City, N.Y., 1958), p. 267. Praz's insistence on the sonnet's base in "a musical principle" is particularly curious in the light of medieval music theory, discussed below, which would have made a musical arrangement well nigh impossible. Praz himself writes, with respect to Wyatt's English sonnets: "The tendency to end the sonnet with a couplet suggested itself *naturally* enough to anyone who overlooked the musical principle (i.e., an even part contrasted with an odd one) on which the sonnet was based" [italics mine] (p. 268). Praz seems here to recognize, albeit inadvertently, that the form may not have been intended for music. I take up this issue below.

ment and derives from a tradition of performed and sung poetry),
may in fact be indulging in mere wishful, and ultimately not interesting, thinking, in which certain unique aspects of the form are
largely ignored.

The most obvious fact about the sonnet as a form is that it
moves not toward but away from an already existing song form,
the *strambotto,* through the addition of the sestet, and thus becomes something new, attractive, and mysterious.[12] Nor is the
new form in any sense "typical" of those invented by the troubadours, and perfected by them before listening audiences. For one
thing, although the sestet, in most of the manuscripts of Giacomo's
sonnets, is set off by an initial capital from the octave, no excep-
tional interlinear space occurs between the two units: the fourteen
lines appear therefore as a single major unit on the page, within
which a (usually single) capital letter indicates the ninth line. The
ninth line is further indicated by the placing of the first word of
lines one and nine somewhat to the left of the first words of each
of the other lines within the poem, or stanza. And it is, from one
point of view at least, a stanza, an independent stanza, that we are
looking at when we look at any sonnet—a stanza with a twist, a
sudden turn of thought, an abrupt transformation of theme, in the
middle, at line nine. No such break occurs, so far as I can deter-
mine, in any of the stanzas of any of the *canzoni* of any of the
troubadours. On the contrary, the very notion of "stanza" in troubadour songs implies, as Maurice Valency has pointed out, the
presence of an intricate, thematically coherent thought whose verbal structure matches perfectly its accompanying and similarly
complete musical structure:

12. The "newness," or even "uniqueness," of the form—its essential "difference" from other forms—is, I maintain, something that both Giacomo
and his contemporaries sensed from the start. But in fact it was by no means
unusual for Giacomo to "invent" forms. As Wilkins notes, he was a tech-
nical innovator. Perhaps he was such by nature, a kind of Picasso of poetics,
whose inventiveness occasionally exceeded his gifts of expression. In any
event, it is worth observing with Wilkins that *each* of Giacomo's twenty-
two *canzoni* is individual and unique in form. What must also be added at
this point is that the fourteen-line sonnet as invented by Giacomo does not
consist of an eight-line *strambotto* to which Giacomo added a six-line *strambotto*—or of the addition of one musical form to another. On the disproof
of this possibility, see Wilkins, "Invention," pp. 493–94.

By the end of the twelfth century, the term *chanson*, in Provençal *canso* or *chanso*, had come to mean a love-song of some half-dozen stanzas of identical structure, usually, but not always, set to a new melody, a melody especially composed for it. The *chanson*, like the liturgical hymn, was in general monostrophic—each strophe was meant to be sung to the same tune—and the stanzas were consequently matched with great exactness, line for line, syllable for syllable. The musical thought of the *chanson* was thus completely contained within the single stanza, and each stanza was an independent unit of song. . . . In the lyric, a new departure was ordinarily made with each stanza, the logical links between stanza and stanza were weak or lacking, and the effect is of a recurrence rather than a progression.[13]

But the earliest sonnets of Giacomo, which appear in the manuscripts as single stanzas treated as separate poems and contain turns of thought following line eight, clearly fly in the face of this established practice of the troubadours. What is more, the question of composing music for the sonnet, along the traditional lines of the *formes fixes* and the *cantus firmus* techniques, so common in Giacomo's time, would appear to be complicated by the lopsided structure of the sonnet.[14] The six lines of the sestet hardly match

13. *In Praise of Love* (New York, 1958), p. 118.
14. That the change in the stanzaic structure of the sonnet, occurring after line eight, would have produced an insoluble problem for the medieval composer is suggested by these remarks of Edward E. Lowinsky in his important essay "Music in Renaissance Culture": "Medieval music was not only based in preexisting melodies, it was *formally and rhythmically fitted to ready made patterns*. . . . It is difficult to imagine that the musician of the Renaissance would break out from the safety of the *formes fixes* and the *cantus firmus* technique into a freedom of expression in which all guidance and direction was lacking" (*Journal of the History of Ideas*, 15 (1954), 529, 535). Obviously it would have been perfectly possible to write *bad* music for sonnets in the Middle Ages, simply by ignoring the structural change after line eight, and repeating whatever melodic order had been established. I maintain, however, that based on the evidence this is extremely unlikely: indeed, it probably did not happen. The stanzaic structure of the sonnet and the prevailing approaches to musical composition are too much at variance to facilitate a happy combination—or even a sad one—of the two. Lowinsky observes that a chief innovation of the Renaissance composer was his decision to produce music that would somehow agree with his texts, with the meanings and moods of the words as well as with the structures of stanzas and structural changes (pp. 535–37). I am grateful to a former student, Jo

in weight and length the eight lines of the octave, though in good
sonnets they summarize and resolve the thematic tensions of the
octave. A composer would find it practically impossible, one might
guess, to compose decently for the sonnet form unless he ignored
the conventions of composition popular in the High Middle Ages.
If on the one hand he were to produce a single melody for the
whole poem, he would do so at the expense of sensitivity to the
turn of thought occurring after line eight; if he were to produce
two different melodies for the poem, a longer one for the octave
and a shorter one for the sestet, he would come up with an
asymmetrical composition completely at variance with what is
known of the traditions of such music.[15] It is therefore perhaps
suggestive that, as Mönch has pointed out (pp. 82–83), no musical settings for Petrarch's sonnets can be assigned a date earlier
than 1470, well over two centuries after Giacomo wrote his first
sonnets: there may simply have been no earlier settings. Mönch's
piece of evidence becomes even more indicative of the possibly
nonmusical nature of the sonnet when we recall that a large number of musical settings for other types of nearly contemporaneous
poetry have survived intact.[16]

Anne Kraus, for bringing Lowinsky's work to my attention. Gustave Reese,
in his study *Music in the Renaissance* (New York, 1954), pp. 156ff., dis-
cusses the practice of setting to music *frottole,* a loose category of lyrics that
included *strambotti,* odes, and occasionally sonnets, in Italy in the seventeenth century. Cf. also Iain Fenlon, "Music and Patronage in Italy, 1450–
1550," in his *Music in Medieval and Early Modern Europe* (Cambridge,
Eng., 1981), pp. 163ff.

15. Valency comments: "The *chanson,* like the liturgical hymn, was in
general monostrophic [by the end of the twelfth century]—each strophe was
meant to be sung to the same tune—and the stanzas were consequently
matched with great exactness, line for line, syllable for syllable" (p. 118).
On the treatment of *divisible* stanzas, Valency writes: "Other stanzas, however, are divisible, and the division—the turn or *diesis*—marks a change of
melody. This change, so Dante tells us, always takes place in connection with
a repetition of the original melody. . . . Where there is repetition of the
melody, of course, the feet must be exactly symmetrical, syllable for syllable,
and so the verses" (p. 119). This last requirement would clearly have elimi-
nated the sonnet from consideration.

16. Lowinsky notes in this connection, "Since the days of Philippe de
Vitry (1291–1361) composers have been known to enter their own names
into the texts which they set to music" (p. 525).

It is at this point that an inquiry into the plausible meanings, origins, and early uses of the word "sonnet" may prove valuable. The first appearances of the word *sonetto* in Italian are conventionally assigned to the latter part of the thirteenth century, and often to the poet Guittone d'Arezzo, one of Giacomo's immediate successors and certainly one of the finer practitioners of the art.[17] But while Guittone may have known the word *sonetto,* and may have understood it as designating a particular poetic form, neither he nor Giacomo uses it anywhere, nor is there evidence that either of them referred to the newly invented form in which they were writing by any special name. Indeed, the word's first appearance as a literary term occurs only at the end of the thirteenth century (1294), in the *Vita nuova* of Dante (where *sonetto* is not so much defined or described as merely offered as a name). The first critical discussion of the sonnet occurs apparently, and perhaps importantly, not in Italian at all but in the Latin of Dante's *De vulgari eloquentia,* that major effort, unfortunately incomplete, to account for the development of language and, in Book II, for the prosody of the *canzone.*[18] Thus it is possible, and perhaps even likely, that the word *sonetto* had gained currency by the start of the fourteenth century, but we have scant evidence of this. What is more, Dante's use of the Latin *sonitus*—it appears twice in Book II of the *De vulgari*—is of enormous value in helping us understand how poets were thinking of the sonnet as a form; even the word *sonitus* itself, given Dante's use of it as equivalent to *sonetto,* must be seen as indicating in its own meanings those earliest meanings, commonly accepted by quite a few poets, including obviously Dante, of the Italian word. It will perhaps be correct to regard *sonitus* as the source of the Italian word and of its meanings.

Dante's use of *sonitus* is clearly disparaging, and this despite the fact that he himself is the author of some of the finest sonnets in

17. See Carlo Battisti and Giovanni Alessio, *Dizionario etimologico italiano* (Florence, 1957), V, 3543. On Guittone's priority, see Fuller, *The Sonnet,* p. 4. The earliest published collection of Guittone's sonnets (1527) refers to them simply as *rime* (*Giuntina di Rime antiche*).

18. Dante's *De vulgari* certainly dates from before 1305. Some thirty years after Dante, Antonio da Tempo provides an instructional manual that describes the various types of sonnets and how to write them. See Antonio da Tempo, *Summa artis rithimici vulgaris dictaminis* (1329–38), critical edn., ed. Richard Andrews (Bologna, 1977).

Italian. In the first of the two places in which he refers to the *sonitus,* he compares it unfavorably to the *canzone,* that noblest of lyrics, as he conceives of it, and to the *ballata,* that type of lyric which is danced as well as sung:

> Adhuc: quicquid per se ipsum efficit illud ad quod factum est, nobilius esse videtur quam quod extrinseco indiget: sed cantiones per se totem quod debent efficiunt, quod ballate non faciunt: indigent enim plausoribus, ad quos edite sunt; ergo cantiones nobiliores ballatis esse sequitur extimandas, et per consequens nobilissimum aliorum esse modum illarum, cum nemo dubitet quin ballate sonitus nobilitate excellant.[19] [Beyond this: anything that creates on its own the effect for which it was made seems more noble than that which needs outside assistance: but *canzoni* create by themselves the entire effect that they should create, which ballads do not do; for they beg for the performers for whom they were written; therefore it follows that *canzoni* are to be judged more noble than ballads, and as a result, the most noble of any form, for no one questions that ballads surpass sonnets in nobility.]

The *canzone,* he wishes to argue, is the most noble of lyrics because it permits the greatest musical and verbal complexities to emerge from the greatest ease of performance: it needs no external assistance, as does the *ballata,* which requires a dance accompaniment of some sort. The *sonitus,* which he barely mentions, is perhaps to be understood as least noble among these forms precisely because it is the least complex—it consists, after all, of just one stanza—and because it requires most "assistance." The "assistance" required may in fact be music (certainly it would not be dance, as that sort of "assistance" was already available with the *ballata*). This notion, that music in Dante's day was conventionally absent from sonnets and sonnet presentations, is rather interestingly supported when we consider more deeply the meaning of the word *sonitus.* The word, in medieval Latin, appears in legal and papal documents as early as the year 817, where it means "murmur," or "soft sound," or merely "soft noise."[20] Behind this

19. Dante Alighieri, *De vulgari eloquentia,* II.iii.5–7, in *Opere minori,* 2nd edn., ed. Alberto del Monte (Milan, 1966), pp. 576–77.

20. See Carolo du Fresne, *Glossarium mediae et infimae latinitatis* (1883–87; rpt. Graz, 1954), p. 527.

medieval sense of the word, which had not, so far as can be seen, altered by Dante's time, lies of course the classical sense of *sonitus,* which was certainly implicit in the word even when Dante used it in the fourteenth century. In classical Latin *sonitus* can mean murmur, but its larger meaning is simply noise, not noise as in music, but noise as in empty sound, bombast, thunder. In his second reference to the *sonitus,* Dante implies—most strongly, it seems—that the presence of actual music and an actual performance may not really be necessary to the making of the "sound" in this type of poem: "Et ideo cantio nichil aliud esse videtur quam actio completa dictantis verba modulationi armonizata: quapropter tam cantiones quas nunc tractamus, quam ballatas et sonitus, et omnia cuiusconque modi verba sunt armonizata vulgariter et regulariter, cantiones esse dicemus."[21] [And therefore a *canzone* appears to be nothing but the finished act of writing down the harmonized words according to their rhythms: for this reason we shall call *canzoni* not only those poems we are now discussing, but also ballads and sonnets, and all words, of whatever sort, that are harmonized, whether in the vulgar language or in Latin.] The key word in this passage is "armonizata." It can mean—and so it has usually been understood—"set to music"; but it has also the more general meaning of "harmonized," and it is in this sense, of words arranged in metrical and rhyming harmonies, whether with or without music, that Dante seems to want us to take it: for the purpose of the passage is basically to demonstrate that while any *canzone* may attract a musical accompaniment (and Dante wishes to include the *sonitus* as a subcategory among the *canzoni*), no music by itself may be regarded as a *canzone:* it must have lyrics. The issue of the sonnet as a stanza perhaps to be set to music is therefore, as Dante presents it, admittedly ambiguous: sonnets may or may not be like all the other medieval lyrics, which invariably had musical accompaniments. The weight of such evidence as exists, however, appears to favor most heavily the notion that sonnets did not—at least not necessarily—come equipped with music, or seek it, and indeed that the poet himself was probably unacquainted with any sonnets that had been set to music.

21. *De vulgari,* II.viii.6–7, pp. 593–94.

Giacomo's earliest sonnets themselves provide the strongest clues to the possibility that in writing them the poet was deliberately turning away from the kinds of songs made and sung by the troubadours and creating a new type of lyric with new, "modern," and silent intentions. Langley, whose 1915 edition of *The Poetry of Giacomo da Lentino* remains the authority on his poetry, attributes twenty-six sonnets definitely to Giacomo, while including three that are probably authentic and nine that must be regarded as unauthentic.[22] I would like to consider one of these, sonnet XI. Wilkins, indulging in a bit of guesswork, suggests that while sonnet XI may be less polished and masterful than others, it may, on grounds of sheer primitivism, perhaps be the poet's first, or as is likely, the first sonnet ever written.[23] Sonnet XI, at any rate, offers salient points of interest, or clues, which are pertinent to this investigation and are typical also of all of Giacomo's other sonnets:

Molti amadori la lor malatia
    portano in core, che 'm vista nom pare;
    ed io nom posso sì celar la mia
    ch' ella nom paia per lo mio penare;
    però che son sotto altrui segnoria,
    nè di meve non ò neiente a fare,
    se non quanto madonna mia voria,
    ch' ella mi pote morte e vita dare.
Su' è lo core, e suo sono tutto quanto,
    e chi non à comsiglio da suo core,
    non vive imfra la gente como deve.
    Càd io nom sono mio nè più nè tanto,
    se non quanto madonna è de mi fore,
    ed un poco di spirito ch' è 'n meve.[24]

Certain themes, such as the concept of love as a sickness ("malatia") and the notion that the lady possesses immense power over the very life of the lover ("ch' ella mi pote morte e vita dare"), are common in the love songs of the troubadours and undoubtedly reflect Giacomo's indebtedness to them. But one is struck from the first by the absence of two elements essential to successful per-

---

22. Ernest F. Langley, ed., *The Poetry of Giacomo da Lentino, Sicilian Poet of the Thirteenth Century* (Cambridge, Mass., 1916), pp. x–xi.

23. Wilkins, "Invention," p. 494.

24. Langley, *Poetry,* p. 69. Cf. my translation, p. 53.

formed poetry and ubiquitous in troubadour poetry: the absence of any even implied address to a listening audience, and the absence of multiple or dual personae—what W. T. H. Jackson has called the "love-persona," or the persona who actually suffers the pains of unrequited love, and the "poet-persona," who makes the song.[25] Giacomo's poem is of course not addressed in any sense to "the Lady" whom he loves. If it is addressed to anyone at all, it is to the poet himself; but this view, in which the poet must be seen as engaging in some sort of monologue in isolation, does not do justice to the brevity of the form and the meditative tone of the last line: "ed un poco di spirito ch' è 'n meve." In fact, the poem itself makes the impression of a meditation; and it may be addressed, as I shall try to show, to the very form in which it is written.

What is remarkable, moreover, about sonnet XI—and it is this, one suspects, which more than anything sets the poem apart from those treatments of love to be found in the songs of the troubadours—is its dialectical structure: the fact, treated as an obvious feature of all important sonnets since Giacomo by all critics who have written about the form, that the problem in love presented in the octave is resolved in some fashion in the sestet. The poem is argumentative in nature, and this *within* its single stanza: in the octave we learn of the love-persona's difficulty, that he cannot conceal the *malatia* which results from his devotion to a lady who will have nothing to do with him and who has the power to kill him with her indifference; and in the sestet we, along with the love-persona, find the solution: it lies in the love-persona's (one is tempted to say, the poet's) acceptance of his own humanity, of his passionate and affectionate nature, for in doing so he recovers his ability to live among people (the "gente" of l. 11) and to be more fully alive (as is implied by the "spirito ch' è 'n meve" of l. 14). He discovers, therefore, the way out of his predicament neither (as we might expect in a troubadour love song) by appealing to an outside, listening audience nor by appealing to the lady herself: he finds it through a process of dialectical self-confrontation (or as Yeats might put it, through a quarrel with self: the self, or persona, struggling within the poem), and he finds it within him-

25. See Jackson's important article "Persona and Audience in Two Medieval Love Lyrics," *Mosaic,* 8, no. 4 (Summer 1975), 147–48.

self. Indeed, one senses in many of Giacomo's sonnets that the
man and the love-persona of the poem have blended, achieving an
intimacy, and a psychology, not sought by the troubadours. The
love problem may thus be seen as immediately capable of solution
once it achieves the sonnet form which Giacomo is inventing, and
the persona of the poem, realizing this, addresses himself not to
any outsider but to the form itself. The form of the poem will
solve the problem, and render superfluous the need, found in more
conventional songs, for the persona to split into rival personae.
This is a new and, I would maintain, perhaps even profound development in the "modern" poetry of the West, suggestive of those
tendencies toward introspection in search of form which, it is fair
to say, have guided many of the best poets ever since. Certainly it
marks a turning point in the history of the lyric—away from the
poem as pure public performance, away even from the poem as a
musically accompanied set of mere stanzas. It may not be altogether out of place to speculate that Giacomo, and those early
sonneteers who followed him, felt it necessary to dispense with
"heard melodies" precisely because, from the point of view of
sonnets as meditations, "those unheard" are "sweeter."[26]

26. A certain amount of evidence from succeeding centuries, even from
centuries in which it had become not uncommon to set sonnets to music,
suggests that most people regarded the form as one that required no musical
accompaniment and was not generally thought of in connection with music.
Benvenuto Cellini (1500–1571) speaks at least six times, in his autobiogra-
phy, of sonnets and how they were composed, published, and received. A
number of these passages are perhaps worth citing here in support of my
argument against the sonnet as a necessarily musical form:

> "When this reception was over, we found the whole room full of
> sonnets, which every man of us had made and sent to Michel Angolo.
> My lad began to read them, and read them all aloud so gracefully,
> that his infinite charms were heightened beyond the powers of lan-
> guage to describe." *La vita di Benvenuto Cellini, scritta da lui
> medesimo,* ed. B. Bianchi (Florence, 1852), I, xxx, 61; trans. John
> Addington Symonds.

> "So then Bandinello began to chatter, and cried out: 'Prince, when I
> uncovered my Hercules and Cacus, I verily believe a hundred sonnets
> were written on me, full of the worst abuse which could be invented
> by the ignorant rabble.' " (II, lxx, 414)

> "Now it pleased God that, on the instant of its exposure to view, a
> shout of boundless enthusiasm went up in commendation of my work,

It is not in the end surprising to find that the earliest sonnets, if they are to be seen as the formal meditations which the evidence seems to show them to be, were written by a "notary" in the service of Frederick II. *Notaro* in Giacomo's day meant "lawyer" as well as "notary," and in Giacomo's case this meant a very important lawyer indeed—apparently with direct access to the most brilliant, intellectual, and literary emperor of the age.[27] That such a "notary," rather than either a troubadour or a minstrel, should produce a poetic form which is simultaneously dialectical and introspective should perhaps be regarded as only appropriate. The nature of the new lyric, the sonnet, with its capacity for self-confrontation, corresponds perfectly to the questioning, "modern" spirit of Frederick's own life and career, in which accepted forms and modes of thought, including those of the Church itself, were subjected to constant challenge. M. Schipa's comments on Fred-

---

which consoled me not a little. The folk kept on attaching sonnets to the posts of the door, which was protected with a curtain, while I gave the last touches to the statue. I believe that on the same day when I opened it a few hours to the public, more than twenty were nailed up, all of them overflowing with the highest panegyrics. Afterwards, when I once more shut it off from view, every day brought sonnets, with Latin and Greek verses; for the University of Pisa was then on vacation, and all the doctors and scholars kept vying with each other who could praise it best. But what gratified me most, and inspired me with most hope of the Duke's support, was that the artists, sculptors and painters alike, entered into the same generous competition. I set the highest value on the eulogies of that excellent painter Jacopo Pontormo, and still more on those of his able pupil Bronzino, who was not satisfied with merely publishing his verses, but sent them by his lad Sandrino's hand to my house. They spoke generously of my performance, in that fine style of his which is most exquisite, and this alone repaid me somewhat for the pain of my long troubles." (II, xc, 454)

In these and other places Cellini, who never speaks of the sonnet as in any way associated with music, constantly refers to it as an epistle, a meditation, a poem of public praise (but chiefly intended for silent reading), and as a poem of scorn or satire.

27. The essential biography of Frederick remains Ernst Kantorowicz's *Frederick the Second,* trans. E. O. Lorimer (1931; rept. New York, 1957), though Kantorowicz incorrectly attributes the invention of the sonnet to Pier della Vigna. On the enormously important roles played by poets and poetry at the court of Frederick II, see Kantorowicz, pp. 328–34.

erick ought, for the sake of context, to be placed alongside Giacomo's accomplishment as the poet who invented the sonnet:

> It is not difficult to make a list of Frederick's astonishing qualities:
> how this Italian Hohenstaufen was the heir and embodiment of three
> civilisations—Saracenic, Byzantine, western medieval—how his tal-
> ents ranged in mastery over law, administration, war, diplomacy,
> philosophy, precocious science, poetry, and art. . . . It is easy, too,
> to sum up his achievements: that by his all but successful resistance
> and his constant appeal to public opinion in manifestoes and letters
> he undermined the political prestige of the Papacy; that in the verse-
> making of his courtiers and himself Italian literature took its rise,
> and in his building and magnificence lay for the fine arts the fertile
> seeds of a new era; and that with his Byzantine and Norman inheri-
> tance he created "the state as a work of art."[28]

It is in this context of reason, curiosity, and challenges to established models, whether in politics, on the battlefield, or in the arts,
that the earliest sonnets make their appearance. One suspects not
only that this is no accident but that the invention of the sonnet
must itself be considered symptomatic of the slowly developing
state of mind that we designate by the term "Renaissance."

The chief conclusions to be reached, therefore, are first, that the
usual view that all medieval lyrics had musical accompaniments
and were performed before audiences has, at least as far as the
sonnet is concerned, no basis in fact. Most of the music we possess
for the sonnet dates from well over two hundred years subsequent
to the first sonnets of Giacomo da Lentino. When we consider
that a good deal more music for other types of poetry has survived
from Giacomo's time, we are forced to question whether the
earliest sonnets were ever intended for music or public performance—whether they did not indeed represent not only a new
formal tendency in lyric poetry but a new thematic interest as
well. Second, Dante's ambivalence about the word *sonitus*—his
implication that the sounds of sonnets may not necessarily be the
sounds of performed music—reinforces the conviction that the
sonnet, as it was originally conceived, may have been intended

28. "Italy and Sicily under Frederick II," in *Cambridge Medieval History*
(Cambridge, 1957), VI, 165.

less for public displays (in the sense of performance) than for private encounters between reader and poem. Third, Giacomo's earliest sonnets, while revealing an enormous debt to certain troubadour attitudes toward love, break sharply from troubadour poetry in their insertion of a "turn" within a stanza; their dialectical resolution of emotional problems within a single stanza; their assumption that emotions can be clarified through formal logic, and this within a mere fourteen lines; their indifference to a mass audience, or even to an audience of more than one; their reduction of the two personae of troubadour love lyrics to one, apparently that of the suffering lover; and their focus on the persona's ability to solve the problem presented in the octave without recourse to outside help, in other words through the poem itself, in its sestet. Fourth, the cultural and political context of Giacomo's invention of the sonnet—that of the court of Frederick II—together with Giacomo's profession as a *notaro,* or lawyer of considerable importance, seems to coincide perfectly with the creation of the type of poem we have been describing, and even to beg, in a sense, for its creation. It may thus be fair to say that the birth of the sonnet heralds a departure from the tradition of lyrics as performed poems and introduces a new, introspective, quieter mode, a mode that is to dominate the history of Western poetry for at least the next seven centuries.

One important problem remains to be considered: why the fourteen lines, or to put the matter more interestingly, why the uniquely attractive, even compelling, combination of the eight-line *strambotto* with Giacomo's six-line inspiration? Probably no absolutely firm solution is possible. Fuller is skeptical of attempts to discover the logical basis of the sonnet in the syllogism, the Greek choral ode, and the musical gamut (see pp. 2–3). His own suggestions about the likely sources of the form are not, however, ultimately satisfying: "In fact, the sonnet's origins support the idea that the bipartite form is the result of a prosodic sleight-of-hand. The eight lines of closed rhyme produce a certain kind of musical pace which demands repetition. Any expectation of stanzaic continuation is, however, violated by the six lines of interlaced rhyme which follow: the sestet is more tightly organized, and briefer, than the octave and so urges the sonnet to a decisive conclusion" (p. 3). Fuller is unquestionably right that the imbalance between the octave and the sestet not only comes as a surprise but makes the conclusion finally attained all the more "decisive." Nonetheless, one senses a vagueness in this explanation. The sonnet, especially Giacomo's earliest sonnets, is above all a numerically precise poem, whose most striking features are (a) its numerical consistency from poem to poem, and (b) the consistently appearing combination of eight lines with six. It is, one strongly suspects, the numerical relationship—a relationship implied even in those relatively few sonnets which are exceptions to the rules and present us with either more or less than fourteen lines—that provides the mystery. To solve the mystery of the numerical relations, which appears to be a problem of proportion or ratio, by suggesting that the relations between eight and six had important meanings in Giacomo's time, meanings which have persisted through the centuries that followed him, will be to do something toward solving the other mystery of the sonnet's vastly popular structure. Before proposing a solution, however, we must, in all fairness to the aesthetically satisfying momentum present in the shape of Giacomo's sonnets as well as in the Shakespearian variation which involves the concluding couplet, and which of course comes along a good deal later in literary history, include another number in our considerations: the number twelve. For the momentum toward what Fuller has called the decisive conclusion of even Giacomo's sonnets, with their *cde-cde* sestets, is established not simply in the six-line unit taken as a whole, but most powerfully in the final two lines. These seem frequently, and despite appearances and rhyme scheme, to stand off by themselves, and so in a sense to leave the previous twelve lines as a rhetorically and numerically separate unit within the poem: "se non quanto madonna è de mi fore, / ed un poco di spirito ch' è 'n meve." The "within" and "without"—the external, internal—oppositions (the distance of the lady, the nearness of the "spirit"), which are also oppositions of images that contrast, draw the lines away from all the others, and precisely toward that finality which the poem so pleasurably provides. The numbers to be considered, therefore, are not simply eight and six, or six:eight, but six:eight:twelve.[29]

29. A question to be asked, too, is not why there is a couplet in the English, or Shakespearian, sonnet, but why there is none in the Italian. It would seem an inevitable consequence of Giacomo's invention that the

In fact these numbers do possess the importance we are looking for. The proportions 6:8 and 6:8:12 did play exceedingly interesting roles in the history of ideas, not merely in Giacomo's time but in the Renaissance, and most particularly in Renaissance architecture, where they describe the "harmonic" proportions of rooms. More than this, the notion of the 6:8:12 relation as "harmonic," and therefore as reflecting what Georgi in his *Harmonia mundi* calls the "fabric of the soul," according to which "the whole world was arranged and perfected," may be found much earlier, in the Pythagorean-Platonic theory of numbers.[30] Rudolf Wittkower writes: "In the wake of the Pythagoreans, Plato in his *Timaeus* explained that cosmic order and cosmic harmony are contained in certain numbers. Plato found this harmony in the squares and cubes of the double and triple proportion starting from unity. . . . The ratios between these numbers contain not only all the musical consonances, but also the inaudible music of the heavens and the structure of the human soul" (p. 104). In writing on "harmonic proportions," albeit with reference to the architectural theories of Palladio (sixteenth century), Wittkower describes the 6:8:12 relation in a manner that bears directly on the earlier-established structure of the sonnet:

> What we now call three terms in "harmonic" proportion is defined in the *Timaeus* (36) as "the mean exceeding one extreme and being exceeded by the other by the same fraction of the extremes." In other words, three terms are in "harmonic" proportion when the distance of the two extremes from the mean is the same fraction of their own quantity (i.e. $\frac{b-a}{a} = \frac{c-b}{c}$). In Palladio's example 6:8:12 the mean 8 exceeds 6 by 1/3 of 6 and is exceeded by 12 by 1/3 of 12 (i.e. $\frac{8-6}{6} = \frac{12-8}{12}$). (pp. 109–10)

There is, of course, no way of being completely certain whether Giacomo da Lentino, in writing his first sonnets, was thinking precisely along the lines of Pythagorean-Platonic number theory pro-

---

couplet-variant be introduced. Mario Praz appears to recognize the issue as significant in his comments quoted in note 11, above.

30. See Rudolf Wittkower, *Architectural Principles in the Age of Humanism* (New York, 1971), p. 104, who advances these notions and quotes extensively from Georgi's work; hereafter cited in the text.

posed here. Whether he was or not, the following is clear. First, the proper ratios for "harmonic" proportions are present in the structure of the new sort of poem, the sonnet, which Giacomo invented, and which therefore should be viewed as a three-dimensional, or architectural, structure. Second, the Pythagorean-Platonic theory of numbers was by no means unfamiliar to educated people, and especially to intellectuals, in Giacomo's day: Giacomo, as noted earlier, figured significantly at what must be regarded as the most intellectual of the European courts of the thirteenth century, that of Frederick II.[31] Third, it is most likely therefore that Giacomo's very training as a lawyer, plus his desire to write a type of lyric which would differ markedly from what had come before it—that would be, in a real sense, a lyric sung by the soul to the soul, in the silent music of the soul—led him, perhaps unconsciously at first, to create a structure in his sonnets that would echo those celestial and silent proportions and ratios described by Plato. In making the first European lyric intended for silent, personal performance, Giacomo constructed it according to the architecture of the soul and of heaven, and set it to the music of the spheres.

31. Kantorowicz argues that we should not hesitate to ascribe intimate knowledge of at least Plato's *Timaeus* both to Frederick himself and to the better-educated members of his court (pp. 338–39). It is, of course, the *Timaeus* whose mathematical ideas are crucial to the notions advanced at this point. Excellent tangential studies of the relations of numbers, ratios, and geometry to subsequent literature, together with the Pythagorean-Platonic influence on Renaissance literature, especially in England, are to be found in Alastair Fowler, *Silent Poetry: Essays in Numerological Analysis* (London, 1970), and his *Triumphal Forms: Structural Patterns in Elizabethan Poetry* (Cambridge, Eng., 1970).

Bibliography

PRIMARY SOURCES

Battisti, Carlo, and Giovanni Alessio. *Dizionario etimologico italiano*. Florence: 1957.

du Bellay, Joachim. *Les Antiquités de Rome* et *Les Regrets*. Paris: 1945.

Boscán, Juan. *Obras poéticas*. Barcelona: 1957.

Bürger, Gottfried August. *Gedichte*. Ed. E. Consentius. Berlin: 1914.

Cellini, Benvenuto. *La vita di Benvenuto Cellini, scritta da lui medesimo*. Ed. B. Bianchi. Florence: 1852.

Dante Alighieri. *Opere minori*. 2nd ed. Ed. Alberto del Monte. Milan: 1966.

Darío, Rubén. *Poesía*. Ed. Ernesto Mejía Sanchez. Caracas: 1977.

Fredericus II. *De arte venandi cum avibus*. Codex Ms. Pal. Lat. 1071 der Biblioteca Apostolica Vaticana. Graz: Akademische Druck- u. Verlagsanstalt, 1969.

Fresne, Carolo du. *Glossarium mediae et infimae latinitatis*. Paris: 1883–1887; rpt. Graz: 1954.

Goethe, Johann Wolfgang von. *Goethes sämmtliche Werke*. 40 vols. Stuttgart: 1869.

Góngora, Luis de. *Sonetos*. Ed. Birute Ciplijauskaite. Madison, Wis.: 1981.

Gryphius, Andreas. *Sonn- und Feiertagssonette* [1639]. Ed. M. Welti. Halle: 1883.

―――. *Gedichte*. Ed. H. Palm. Tübingen: 1884.

Guittone d'Arezzo. *Le Rime*. Ed. F. Egidi. Bari: 1940.

Heine, Heinrich. *Werke*. 7 vols. Ed. Ernst Elster. Leipzig: 1924.

Huch, Ricarda. *Gesammte Gedichte*. Leipzig: 1929.

Ibarbourou, Juana. *Las lenguas de diamante*. Montevideo: 1919.

Jeanroy, Alfred, ed., *Les Poésies de Cercamon*. Paris: 1922.

Kaschnitz, Marie Louise. *Gedichte*. Hamburg: 1947.

―――. *Totentanz und Gedichte zur Zeit*. Hamburg: 1947.

Langley, Ernest F., ed. *The Poetry of Giacomo da Lentino, Sicilian Poet of the Thirteenth Century*. Cambridge, Mass.: 1916.

191

Lope de Vega. *Poesía selecta*. Ed. Antonio Carreno. Madrid: 1984.

———. *Obras*. Ed. Marcelino Menendez Pelayo et al. Madrid: 1963–72.

Lorca, Federico García. *Obras completas* Ed. Arturo de Hoyo. Madrid: 1978.

Machado, Antonio. *Antología poética*. 2nd edn. Ed. Luis Cano. Barcelona: 1984.

Michelangelo Buonarroti. *Rime*. Milan: 1960.

Muselli, Vincent. *Points et Contrepoints*. Paris: 1957.

Nerval, Gérard de. *Poésies*. Ed. Albert Béguin. Lausanne: 1944.

Petrarca, Francesco. *Il Petrarca*. Ed. Monsignor Bembo. Venice: 1573.

———. *Il canzonieri*. Ed. Dino Provenzal. Milan: 1954.

Platen, August von. *Sämtliche Werke*. 4 vols. Ed. Max Koch and Erich Petzet. Leipzig: 1909.

Rilke, Rainer Maria. *Gesammelte Werke*. 6 vols. Leipzig: 1929.

Ronsard, Pierre de. *Oeuvres complètes*. 2 vols. Ed. G. Cohen. Paris: 1938.

Samain, Albert. *Au jardin de l'infante*. Paris: n.d.

Sanguineti, Edoardo, and Giovanni Getto, eds. *Il Sonetto. Cinquecento sonetti dal Duecento al Novecento*. Milan: 1957.

———. *Sonetti della scuola siciliana*. Turin: 1965.

Scève, Maurice. *Oeuvres complètes*. Ed. P. Quignard. Paris: 1974.

Smith, G. Gregory, ed. *Elizabethan Critical Essays*. Oxford: 1904.

Tempo, Antonio da. *Summa artis rithimici vulgaris dictaminis*. Ed. Richard Andrews. Bologna: 1977.

Trakl, Georg. *Gesamtausgabe*. Ed. K. Horwitz. Zurich: 1946.

Unamuno, Miguel de. *Rosario de Sonetos Líricos*. Madrid: 1911.

Valéry, Paul. *Oeuvres*. Paris: 1957.

Wiese, Benno von, and Theodor Echtermeyer, eds. *Deutsche Gedichte: Von den Anfängen bis zur Gegenwart*. Düsseldorf: 1960.

Witte, Karl. *Hundert Sonette von Eugen Baron von Vaerst und zwei Freunden*. Breslau: 1825.

Zeumer, K. *Quellensammlung zur Geschichte der deutschen Reichsverfassung im Mittelalter und Neuzeit*. Leipzig: 1913.

SECONDARY SOURCES

Auerbach, Erich. *Literary Language and its Public in Late Latin Antiquity and in the Middle Ages*. New York: 1965.

Blackmur, Richard P. "Notes on E. E. Cummings' Language." In *Form and Value in Modern Poetry*. New York: 1957, pp. 287–312.

van Cleve, Thomas Curtis. *The Emperor Frederick II of Hohenstaufen.* Oxford: 1972.

Fenlon, Iain. "Music and Patronage in Italy, 1450–1550." In *Music in Medieval and Early Modern Europe.* Cambridge, Eng.: 1981, pp. 163–248.

Fichter, W. L. "Recent Research on Lope de Vega's Sonnets." *Hispanic Review,* VI, no. 1 (1938), 21–34.

Fowler, Alastair. *Silent Poetry: Essays in Numerological Analysis.* London: 1970.

———. *Triumphal Forms: Structural Patterns in Elizabethan Poetry.* Cambridge, Eng.: 1970.

Fuller, John. *The Sonnet.* London: 1972.

Gauclère, Y. *Rimbaud.* Paris: 1950.

Goldin, Frederick. *The Mirror of Narcissus in the Courtly Love Lyric.* Ithaca, N.Y.: 1967.

Hollander, Robert. "Dante and the Martial Epic." Paper delivered at the annual meeting of the Dante Society of America, Modern Language Association, New York, December 1986.

Howell, A. G. Ferrers. *A Translation of the Latin Works of Dante Alighieri.* London: 1904.

Hunt, Leigh, and S. Adams Lee, eds. *The Book of the Sonnet.* Boston: 1867.

Jackson, W. T. H. "Persona and Audience in Two Medieval Love Lyrics." *Mosaic,* 8, no. 4 (Summer, 1975), 147–59.

Jasinski, Max. *Histoire du Sonnet en France.* 1903; rpt. Geneva: 1970.

Jörder, Otto. "Die Formen des Sonetts von Lope de Vega." *Beihefte zur Zeitschrift für romanische Philologie.* 86. Saale: 1936.

Kantorowicz, Ernst F. *Frederick the Second.* Trans. E. O. Lorimer. New York: 1931.

Labé, Louise. *Sonnets.* Trans. Graham Dunstan Martin, with a commentary by Peter Sharratt. Austin: 1972.

Lewis, C. S. *The Discarded Image.* Cambridge, Eng.: 1965.

Lowinsky, Edward E. "Music in Renaissance Culture." *Journal of the History of Ideas,* 15 (1954), 529–37.

Mönch, Walter. *Das Sonett: Gestalt und Geschichte.* Heidelberg: 1955.

Nichols, Stephen G., Jr. "The Medieval Lyric and its Public." *Medievalia et Humanistica,* n.s., no. 3. Cleveland: 1972, pp. 133–54.

Pelizzari, A. *La vita e le opere di Guittone d'Arezzo.* Pisa: 1907.

Powell, James M. *The Liber Augustalis, or Constitutions of Melfi Promulgated by the Emperor Frederick II for the Kingdom of Sicily in 1231.* Syracuse, N.Y.: 1971.

Praz, Mario. *The Flaming Heart.* Garden City, N.Y.: 1958.

Reese, Gustave. *Music in the Renaissance.* New York: 1954.

Rossetti, Dante Gabriel. *The Early Italian Poets, together with Dante's Vita nuova.* London: 1904.

Scarfe, F. *The Art of Paul Valéry.* London: 1954.

Schipa, M. "Italy and Sicily under Frederick II." *Cambridge Medieval History.* J. R. Tanner, C. W. Previté-Orton, and Z. N. Brooke, eds. Cambridge, Eng.: 1957, VI, 131–65.

Smith, Robert Holland. *The Death of Classical Paganism.* New York: 1976.

Valency, Maurice. *In Praise of Love.* New York: 1958.

Welti, H. *Geschichte des Sonettes in der deutschen Dichtung.* Leipzig: 1884.

Wilkins, Ernest Hatch. "The Invention of the Sonnet," *Modern Philology,* 13 (1915), 463–94.

————. *The Invention of the Sonnet and Other Studies in Italian Literature.* Rome: 1959.

Winegarten, Renee. *French Lyric Poetry in the Age of Malherbe.* Manchester, Eng.: 1954.

Wittkower, Rudolf. *Architectural Principles in the Age of Humanism.* New York: 1971.

Wood, C. A., and F. M. Fyfe, eds. and trans. *Friderici Romanorum Imperatoris secundi: De arte venandi cum avibus.* Boston and London: 1955.

Index

Abel: in sonnet of Lorca, 124, 125; discussed, 168

"A Bicycle Built for Two": persona in popular lyrics, 30. *See also* Persona

"Adán" ("Adam"). *See* Lorca, Federico García

Alcione. See D'Annunzio, Gabriele

Aleixandre, Vicente: 167

Alexandria: 6

Alexandrine: influence of Ronsard's use of, 159, 163; as opposed to *vers commun,* 159; importance to German sonneteers, 159; use by Andreas Gryphius, 159; importance to French sonneteers, 163; as natural in French, 163. *See also* Gryphius, Andreas; Ronsard, Pierre de; Huch, Ricarda

Allegory: medieval, 9–10; possible source of, 9; historical shift from, 27

Alonso, Dámaso: 167

Also Sprach Zarathustra. See Nietzsche, Friedrich

Amalécyte: 124, 125; described, 164

Ambrose, Saint: and reading, 24–25. *See also* Reading

Amours de Cassandre. See Ronsard, Pierre de

Amours de Marie. See Ronsard, Pierre de

Amsterdam: 159. *See also* Weckherlin, Georg Rudolf

Angels: medieval conception of, 6

Annunciation: 6; Feast of the, 167

Ansbach: as birthplace of August von Platen, 161

Anselm, Saint: 6

Antaeus: 124, 125; discussed, 164

Antéros: in sonnets of Nerval, 124–25; discussed, 164

Apollinaire, Guillaume: 166

Apollo: in sonnet of Rilke, 110–11

Apulia: castles in, 20

Arabic: 13, 22

Arabs: in medieval Sicily, 14, 171

Archangel: insignificance of at Annunciation, 16. *See also* Annunciation

Ardi: character in *Alcione,* 80–81; noted, 159

Ariadne: alluded to, 141; crown of, 167

Ariosto: Petrarch's influence on, 157. *See also* Petrarch

Aristotle: and physics, 6; idea of "natural" descending order in universe, 7; *Physics,* 15; idea of species in work of, 15; challenged, 21; *Rhetorica,* 22

Athena: role in *Odyssey,* 11

Athens: in Icarus myth, 159

Audience: for sonnets, 3, 12, 124, 174, 182–84, 186–87, 190; for courtly love lyrics, 4–5, 27, 174, 176, 183; for allegory, 9; for Dante's *Commedia,* 37–39

Auerbach, Erich: on Dante, 37

Augustine, Saint: on reason, 4; *City of God (Civitas Dei),* 23; *Confessions,* 24